Discovering Antiques

BY THE SAME AUTHOR

Country Furniture (English Country Furniture in USA)
Treen and Other Turned Woodware for Collectors

Discovering Antiques

Where to Look, What to Look For, How to Restore

Jane Toller

DAVID & CHARLES
Newton Abbot · London · Vancouver

ISBN o 7153 7073 1

Set in 11 on 13pt Imprint
and printed in Great Britain
by Latimer Trend & Company Ltd Plymouth
for David & Charles (Holdings) Limited
South Devon House   Newton Abbot   Devon

Published in Canada
by Douglas David & Charles Limited
132 Philip Avenue   North Vancouver   BC

Contents

List of Illustrations

Apart from where otherwise stated, all illustrations belong to the author

Introduction

This book was written with three main objects in view. Firstly, to point out that there are still discoveries to be made in the antique world, provided the searcher knows enough to recognise them however heavily disguised. Secondly, to show what forms these disguises may take, and how to deal with them, in order to reveal the beauty of the original object. Thirdly, since sometimes antique treasures are missed because of lack of knowledge of specialised subjects, to give short histories of the various items. At the end of the book there is a list of books for further reading.

From long experience in handling antiques both for business and for pleasure, I know that many treasures have been lost to posterity through being thrown away, put on the bonfire, allowed to fall to pieces out-of-doors, given to young children to play with, sent to jumble sales, or pushed out of sight in dark corners, where moths and wood worm have been only too pleased to make them their home. Examples of such losses have been given in some of the other books I have written, and it has been rewarding to receive grateful letters from readers who, acting on the advice given them, have made worthwhile discoveries for themselves. This book includes several more real-life discoveries, and I sincerely hope that these examples may lead to still further lucky finds.

Owing to the steady rise in popularity of antiques these have now come to be in short supply. But it may encourage those interested, to learn that there are still further sources to be explored from which they may find some treasure that will delight them. These finds may not perhaps be of great intrinsic value; but no genuine lover of antiques puts the value of an antique first and foremost, or buys beautiful old things simply as an investment. Such articles were made by craftsmen through the ages to the best of their ability, to supply a need; they have given pleasure to the many generations that have passed, and we naturally want to hand them on in good order to the generations that are to come.

Since beginning this book I have been shown many recent discoveries that have been made by antique lovers. All of them were rescued from what would have been oblivion. I have indeed recently made a few fascinating discoveries myself and have every intention of searching for more. Collecting antiques is indeed an amusing and rewarding pastime for some, and a whole-time occupation for many others.

1 Serendipity-or Discovering Antiques by Accident

It was Horace Walpole who in 1754 coined the word 'serendipity' meaning 'the faculty of making happy and unexpected discoveries by accident'. With this phrase in mind serendipity must be the best word imaginable to head this chapter, which is all about discovering antiques by accident. I have, however, another reason for using it. Some years ago, on a buying trip in Devon, we found ourselves in a small riverside town, at the top end of which there was a small shop where we usually bought one or two nice pieces. On this occasion, having some time on our hands, we continued down the long meandering street to the church, intending to visit it. We found this was impossible as there was a wedding in progress. But a little further down the street we found a hitherto undiscovered antique shop, not yet open to customers. Through the windows we could see many things we needed, and found, on enquiring from the friendly people next door, that the official opening was to be the next day. We returned full of hope on the following morning and were certainly the first customers to enter the shop – which was called 'Serendipity'! It was not a very well-arranged shop, in fact it was not arranged at all. Nothing had been cleaned or polished, but every kind of antique and second-hand article jostled each other in the most hugger-mugger way. Country furniture was there in plenty ranged round the walls. On the floor in fall-overable heaps were antique rugs and ancient carpets. Pictures of every kind – oils, water-colours, prints, engravings, hung on the walls. Brass milk bowls were full of brass candlesticks, wooden cream bowls filled with bits of treen. And, to my joy as a housewife, piles of hand-embroidered tray cloths and runners were placed haphazardly about on chairs. There were china tea-services, Victorian silver knick-knacks, Steven-graphs and Staffordshire figures, brown earthenware casseroles and early iron cauldrons. 'Serendipity' indeed was the right name for such a shop. We bought and bought, and did so well that we never failed to return there whenever we were in the district. And we always managed to find something to make our trip worthwhile.

It would take too long to enumerate all the treasures we found. Perhaps the most rewarding was a large Gothic oak cupboard with the original iron hinges. This had come from the kitchen quarters of a Cornish castle, and had never been coloured or polished except by time and usage. It was the kind of untouched early piece that one dreams about finding, but very rarely does. Oak was not as sought after in those days as it is now, and the other dealers at the sale had not bothered to inspect the kitchens. Mrs Serendipity had done so though, in her search for casseroles and tray cloths. She noticed the cupboard, bid for it, and secured it. We bought it from her and sold it to an eminent collector of early oak who was as delighted to find it as we had been.

But one cannot expect such good luck to last forever. One disappointing day we found the shop closed, with very little in it. The next visit it was empty. 'Serendipity' had departed. Other dealers took it, and we bought from them, but it was never the same, and eventually we ceased going altogether. But in our own home we have one happy discovery from there, to remind us that the whole thing was not a dream. This is an early Eastern rug depicting a mounted horseman with a spotted dog at his heels. It is a constant joy to look at, and a happy reminder of 'Serendipity' and its owner.

Writing about Gothic cupboards reminds me of a beautiful untouched oak one we discovered quite by accident in an old-fashioned upholsterer's in Basingstoke, standing sadly in the window among the plethora of over-stuffed chairs and sofas. Rather unbelievingly we went in to see whether it was genuine, or a miraculously clever fake. This was no fake, and had no place in such a shop. The upholsterer did not know what to do with it. It was not 'my sort of stock at all', he said, and he had only taken it in part exchange to oblige a customer. It was a fine piece, with two doors embellished with Gothic carvings, and seemed to be mutely begging to be removed from such inglorious surroundings. The price to us seemed high, and our resources at that time were small. Regretfully we abandoned it and started walking slowly and then more slowly down the street, talking about it; then, with one accord we turned, fairly ran up the street again straight into the shop, and bought it with no more ado.

In case any reader feels an overpowering desire to visit Basingstoke and seek out this shop with the idea that history might repeat itself, I hasten to say that the shop and the street it was in, and indeed the whole of that part of the town, has all been razed to the ground in the name of progress.

Some years ago we used to go to the environs and suburbs of London to buy. There were places which we visited regularly, one of them being a large emporium in Peckham – a favourite with us as there was easy parking and lots of goods of every possible kind for sale. We rarely came away without a bargain. On one never-to-be-forgotten occasion we had finished our round of this huge establishment, and leaving my husband to settle the bill, I left the shop and started walking back to the car, glancing in the enormous windows as I passed. These were usually laid out as rooms, and one could walk about in them, so we hardly ever stopped to look in the windows from outside. My glance suddenly became fixed on something hanging high up at the side of one of the windows. Hardly daring to believe my eyes I moved closer to examine it, or them rather, for there was another one above it. They were *saladiers* – one of the rarest pieces of treen to be found. A saladier is a wooden chopping-board for raw vegetables, which in itself does not sound very unusual; but it is not just an ordinary board. These particular ones were made of thick walnut measuring about 2ft long and some 15in wide. The tops were beautifully carved with the coats-of-arms of the French families to whom they had belonged. The board below was slightly hollowed out and on each immediately below the carving, a long steel knife was fixed on with a hinge. At the bottom end of the knife was an ornamental steel handle, by which it could be raised, and moved from side to side, as it chopped. I could not get back into the shop quickly enough, but no one else had spotted them in the meanwhile, and we were able to buy them at a very modest price. One of them is in the Pinto Collection of treen in the Birmingham Museum.

That lucky occasion is an example of the fact that, like most eager collectors, I am inclined to go straight into a shop I know well without looking in the windows and then, either from forgetfulness or because one cannot always see into the windows from inside the shop, go out again without another glance, probably missing many good things in doing so. This is a great mistake. One's eagerness should be restrained. But I notice that many of our customers do the same thing, and when I produce something for them to see, confess they had quite forgotten to look in the window.

This emporium we visited at Peckham has another branch about half a mile away. It was at that time the most heavily disguised antique shop I have ever seen. The front, whatever the weather, always seemed to have the sun-blinds down and, hanging in festoons from various hooks on the sides of the door and window, were somewhat grubby sheets, blankets and bedspreads tied up in bundles by the corners. All along in front of the windows were butlers' trays filled with a wonderful selection of kitchen implements and crockery which had seen much better days. But one was not meant to really look in these windows – they were just for throwing a little light on the curious assortment of furniture displayed inside. The antique buyer 'in the know' would walk through the front part of the shop to look for the things he wanted, for every kind of antique was piled up in large rooms at the back. In the very back room of all were carpets and wardrobes, and here there was a door opening on to a flight of steps, which led into a very large yard surrounded by open sheds. This part was given over to somewhat decrepit furniture, iron objects and broken statuary, etc. Right at the end were enclosed railway arches, where office furniture was stored. When seeking antiques we are great believers in 'leaving no stone unturned' or 'any avenue unexplored' so to speak, so we always 'did' the sheds and arches very thoroughly. On one in every half a dozen visits we found something here. And on this memorable day we certainly did so. By some happy accident a new lot of furniture had just been delivered. Among the various miscellaneous pieces were two beautiful 'spoon-back' papier-mâché armchairs in pristine condition, standing out from the background of board-room tables and filing cabinets like a couple of deer in a herd of bison. The chairs were very handsomely decorated with mother-of-pearl and fine gilding. The only trouble was they bore no price ticket. The usual procedure, if unaccompanied by a salesman, was to write one's name on this ticket, thus reserving the object while looking farther afield. But we did not dare to leave the chairs; other people were prowling about and, while we were away, might lay claim to them. So I proceeded to sit on one of the chairs and place my handbag on the other, while my husband did a sort of obstacle race between, round and over the various objects that were for sale, between the railway arches and the proprietor's office which was right at the front of the shop. It seemed a long time before he appeared on the scene again, accompanied by someone bearing a 'sold' label which was duly stuck on the chairs, and I was released from my vigil.

Most collectors and dealers will probably agree with me that sometimes a sort of haze descends which prevents one from recognising the qualities of things one ought to buy. This may be due to tiredness or cold, or the hunger felt when the time for a meal has long since past. I was attacked like this once in a shop in a far-off part of Cornwall. While going through a storeroom to reach another part of the building I noticed, in a hazy sort of way, a very fine oak table base lying on its side on the floor. The four cabriole legs ended in remarkably well-carved hoof feet, but it had no top. I did get as far as asking the price, and was told it was, in that condition, £10. The owner had been trying to find a suitable oak top for it but so far had been unable to do so. This was not surprising as the table was a French one, and the oak was the lovely pale colour used for that particular type of furniture. I passed on without thinking much about it then, but did so afterwards when it was too late to go back. But fate was kind. Months afterwards we visited the same shop and passed the same table, still without a top.

This time I was more alert and examined it thoroughly, then astonished my husband by saying we would like to have it, explaining to him afterwards that we needed a table like that for ourselves. 'What about the top?' he asked. 'If I had had more sense when I saw it before I should have realised that it had originally had a marble top,' I replied. On our return home we managed to secure a suitable marble top for it and it now stands in our own room – a very handsome piece of furniture indeed. I was very lucky to get that second chance (Plate 1).

Not very long ago we bought an early eighteenth-century sampler from a friend who normally buys and sells antique books and documents. It was most beautifully worked, but had been badly framed. Now while we often find late eighteenth-century samplers in their original gilt frames, the seventeenth- and early eighteenth-century ones have been framed in this century or the very last years of the nineteenth because, when they were finished in the earlier days, they were rolled up in the same manner as the original 'samplers' or 'stitch patterns' had been, and put away in drawers or workbaskets, for at this early date no one thought of framing such things. Having removed this sampler from the frame, I made an interesting discovery. The sampler had begun with the name of the embroideress, and the date on which she started it; it is more usual to find this at the end of a sampler. The frame had not been specially made for this one, instead the end of the sampler was folded over about an inch, to make it fit the frame – in that last inch was embroidered the date when it was finished. This was most unusual. I rang up a friend who is a connoisseur of the subject, to tell him about this discovery, and he had never heard of a sampler before that gave both dates. Other experts agreed with him, and he was delighted to acquire something that appears to be unique. (Incidentally, this long and very beautifully embroidered work had been started in July, and finished three months later in October.)

Unless something has been recently framed, or is excessively fragile such as silk needlework, we always take it out of its frame to clean the glass, and remove any dust. It is astonishing what we have discovered during this operation. We once found an oil painting of George Washington used as padding behind the embroidery in an antique firescreen. It was quite a good copy of the original well-known one and, put into another frame, sold very well. Often we have come across the name of the embroideress on the back of the frame itself under the covering paper. And once we found a will, properly signed and witnessed, written round the back of the frame of a large oil painting of an eighteenth-century lady.

One of the things I have found out in my efforts to discover otherwise unheeded antiques, is always to look below as well as above eye-level, in order to see what has been put on low shelves, or even on the floor. Some years ago at a large country fair I was searching for embroidery pictures on a very crowded picture stand, when suddenly my eye was drawn to a pencil sketch of a charming young boy in late eighteenth-century dress. Possibly he had been wearing a new suit when the sketch was made because he had that air of delighted pride that is felt on such an occasion. It was in a very dark corner, standing on the floor with a pile of pictures behind. I picked it up to find it was framed in a most unsuitable Edwardian frame, and that behind it there was another similar picture. Even in the bad light there could be no doubt that both sketches were of very fine workmanship. There was handwriting underneath both portraits which I could not see well enough to read, except to know that it was French. I hurriedly found my husband, who was searching for oak furniture, and brought him to look at the pictures, which we bought unhesitatingly. On later examination we found that the drawings were of two French boys named Alphonse and Alexandre aged seventeen and nineteen. They had enlisted in the French royalist army, and both been killed on the same day in a fight with revolutionaries. We had the sketches, which were about 12in by 18in, cleaned, and framed in something more suitable, and sold them 'to a good home'. But the faces of the boys still haunt me. They looked so fresh and eager, and life must have seemed to them so full of promise. The poor parents, in those eighteenth-century days when no lists of wounded and killed in battle were given, must have waited some time before the tragic news was brought to them. But the news did arrive, because the details of the boys' deaths have been written in beautiful handwriting below each portrait. It would be interesting to know how the portraits came to be in this country, but it will have to remain a mystery – like so many others!

Not all my discoveries have been bought by me, some have been gifts. At first I have not always realised how interesting they were, and have made the happy discovery much later. For instance, an elderly lady, a friend of the family knowing how keen I was on history, was fond of telling me stories of her ancestors, a young couple named Venables, who had been in personal service in the royal household at Windsor and Kew at the start of the nineteenth century. They had a daughter named Augusta in whom the princesses seem to have taken a great interest, giving her quite expensive toys. These had been kept with great care, and handed down in the family until they came to our friend. I have seen them for myself, and told their story in *Living with Antiques*. Because I was extremely interested in her stories she insisted on giving me a *Book of Common Prayer* which had belonged to Edward Venables, and which had his name beautifully inscribed in the front. It was bound in red morocco, and was interesting because it had been published by 'John Reeves Esq' in 1807, and had a lengthy dedication to the queen. As well as the usual contents it contained forms of service, not found in later editions, to be used for commemorating four other solemn occasions. These forms of service were described as follows:

GUNPOWDER TREASON   A form of Prayer with Thanksgiving to be used yearly on the Fifth Day of November, for the happy deliverance of King James I, and the three Estates of England, from the most traitorous and bloody intended Massacre by Gunpowder, and also for the happy Arrival of his Majesty King William on this Day for the deliverance of our Church and Nation (Plate 4).

KING CHARLES THE MARTYR   A form of Prayer with Fasting to be used yearly upon the Thirtieth Day of January, being the Day of the Martyrdom of the Blessed King Charles I, to implore the mercy of God that neither the Guilt of that sacred and innocent Blood, nor those other Sins by which God was provoked to deliver up both us and our King into the hands of cruel and unreasonable Men, may at any time hereafter be visited upon us, or our Posterity.

RESTORATION OF THE ROYAL FAMILY   A form of Prayer with Thanksgiving to Almighty God, for having put an end to the Great Rebellion, by the Restoration of the King and Royal Family, and the Restoration of the Government, after many years interruption; which unspeakable Mercies were wonderfully completed upon the Twentyninth of May, in the year 1660. And in Memory thereof, that day in every year is, by Act of Parliament appointed to be forever kept holy.

THE KING'S ACCESSION   A Form of Prayer with Thanksgiving to Almighty God to be used in Churches and Chaples within this Realm every year, upon the Twenty-fifth day of October, being the day on which his Majesty (George III) began his happy Reign.

The prayer book was well worn, and had two sketches on the end papers, one of a memorial tablet containing military emblems, the other a thumbnail sketch of a lady in a Regency bonnet. Both done no doubt to enliven a lengthy sermon. They were expert little sketches and added to the interest of the book which I carefully put away, with other similar books, on my shelves, and then forgot all about it. Recently I was looking on these same shelves for a book I needed for some particular research, when I came across Edward Venables's book, and took it up and opened it. Then occurred one of those strange moments when an antique suddenly ceases to be something inert from long ago, and takes on a life of its own. I think it was the human touch of the little sketches that made me see it through the owner's eyes so to speak. It had been well used – especially for morning and evening prayer – and I was able to picture it in his hands as he sat in Saint George's Chapel, Windsor, or in the delightful church on Kew Green where the royal family worshipped when in residence at Kew. I felt impelled to learn more about the history of Edward Venables, so that I could write a note about it and leave it in the book for the benefit of future owners. I knew that he had been much in Windsor, so I got in touch with the archivist at the castle and, explaining my reasons for doing so, inquired if the name Edward Venables appeared on any of the Household Lists of the time. I received the following very interesting information:

We have a record of an Edward Venables who was a Page to the younger daughters of George III from June 1804 to October 12th, 1812. From 1812–1816 he is shown in the printed lists of the Royal Household in the Court and City Register as a Page in the Establishment of the Princesses, and finally as a Page to the Household of the Duke and Duchess of Gloucester from 1817–1824. In a letter from Princess Mary to the King she mentions that 'Venables had fallen ill, and cannot help them in their journey from Weymouth to Windsor'.

It seems obvious from this letter that Venables acted in the capacity of equerry on these occasions, arranging matters of transport, etc, when the princesses were travelling.

In the reign of George III alterations were made to Windsor Castle to bring it more up-to-date. During this time the younger princesses with their governess and staff were housed in what was known as 'Lower Lodge'. This house had been built by Charles II for Nell Gwynne, and now belonged to the Duke of St Albans, who sold it to the queen. Edward Venables was employed in the household of the princesses from 1804–16. In 1816 Princess Mary married her cousin the Duke of Gloucester, and significantly we find Edward Venables assigned as page to the household of the Duke and Duchess in 1817 still, one might say, in the service of one of the princesses. In 1824 when he retired, he settled down near Kew and occupied his time in drawing and painting, for which he had great talent.

The story our old friend had told me of her ancestors, had seemed at the time to be a romantic legend that had been handed down in the family. Now the legend is an accredited fact, and Edward Venables's prayer book will be preserved by me, together with its history and the written authority from the Windsor archives.

Wherever possible those who possess similar legendary articles should try by some means to get them authenticated. I know this may be difficult, but one thing at least almost anybody with old family portraits can do, that is to write the names and dates of the subject in indelible ink on the back. Hundreds of portraits go unidentified because this simple job has not been done. I have often heard old people saying, 'that was my great-aunt Sarah, or my great-great grandfather Sir . . .'. Their younger relations may not be particularly interested, or just forgetful, so a great deal of information interesting and helpful to the historian is lost. And a well-painted portrait may lose value because there is no written history attached to it.

Another piece of advice is to keep any papers relating to the authenticity of valuable historic property in a bank. It is not wise to keep them in the house – a copy, by all means, but not the original. I feel very strongly about this, and will explain why. When I was doing my training in antiques and interior decorating, a lady and her son came into the shop one day and offered for sale an object which had been carefully preserved ever since it had come into the family's possession. It was a 'thumb rosary' that had belonged to Charles I, who had given it on the scaffold to his doctor. It had been handed down ever since in the female line from mother to daughter. (A 'thumb rosary' shows only the last decade of the rosary and the crucifix. At the opposite end is a ring to fit over the thumb, and the rest of the rosary can be kept concealed in the hand.) There had been old letters and papers which proved its authenticity, but they were not kept in a fire-proof safe, and the house of the rosary's present owner had been recently burnt to the ground. She had managed to escape with a few valuables, one of them being the rosary, but all the papers proving its authenticity had perished in the fire. She was hard up, there was no daughter to hand it on to, so very reluctantly she and her son decided they must sell the precious relic. It had been offered to several museums who were very interested, but all required documentation. She had sworn an affidavit that the necessary papers had been destroyed by fire, but this availed nothing. No one doubted the story, for it had the ring of truth, and there was no doubt about the rosary being the right age, for it was proved to be of seventeenth-century workmanship. But no one would offer to pay more than its intrinsic value, not what it would have been worth as an extremely interesting historic relic. I have often wondered what happened to it eventually.

I was interested because I possess a Stuart relic myself – a small silver-gilt oval box. The lid forms the frame for a medal Charles had struck for his adherents while he was at Oxford. It was his head in relief on one side, and that of his queen, Henrietta Maria, on the other. This box without doubt was made to hold some small memento of the king and was given to me simply because the donor had learnt that I had Stuart blood in my veins! Whatever it had contained had disappeared years before.

I suppose the really dedicated searcher for antiques never loses hope of finding such treasures 'by accident'. I know that I never do. We visit very many places where such things might be found in the course of a year, and on the threshold of each one I feel the same stab of excitement – the same thrill of the chase!

2 Antiques Disguised Under Coats of Varnish

Some time in the early part of this century a cheap and nasty type of dark brown varnish came on to the market. It was easily and quickly applied, and had a hard bright look when dry. This was used by amateurs when attempting to give a new look to worn-out second-hand furniture, and could be recognised from a long way off by its chocolate colour. Unfortunately, it was used not only for second-hand furniture, but on antiques made of light woods in order to make them look like rosewood or mahogany – Regency antiques being highly fashionable in the twenties and thirties. We must have removed gallons of this varnish from pieces of antique furniture, and really enjoyed doing so. It was wonderfully encouraging to see the original colour gradually emerging, and one simply had to go on with the task until it was finished. It was agony to have to leave it to go on to some other employ.

Not only was this varnish used on woods so that they might pass as mahogany, but a darker edition was put out with which to stain oak, to get it to conform to the (then) popular idea of 'Jacobean oak'. Unless oak was really Jacobean, we did not like it dark, and numbers of dressers, chests-of-drawers, gate-leg and other tables, came our way that were made of lighter oak, walnut, fruit wood and even yew-tree, all heavily disguised in this depressing way. But this varnish had one thing in its favour; it chipped off extremely easily, so the process of removing the disguise did not take too long.

When my husband returned to the army during World War II, I was left to do the buying alone, and found quite a lot of these varnished pieces; which was just as well, because buying was an extremely difficult process in those days, especially when it had to be done without benefit of a car. I was running the shop as well as buying, and although I had some help with the house and the baby, my buying time was limited, so I searched all the neighbouring districts with a considerable success. Maidenhead was a favourite spot, as it was an easy bus ride from our shop in Marlow. One day, at the far end of a rather remote side street, I spied a chest-of-drawers which, by its shape, looked like an early one. That it was a mahogany colour, and had only three feet, did not put me off at all, and I proceeded at a fast pace down the street towards it. The piece, looking down-at-heel and dejected stood on the pavement outside a real old-fashioned junk shop. 'Chocolate varnish!' I said to myself, and started chipping off a bit (where it wouldn't show) with my thumb nail. This disclosed, what I had fully expected, the walnut underneath. Concealing my delight, I asked the price from the shopkeeper who had suddenly emerged from the back of the shop down a passage fringed with derelict gas stoves. 'That old chest,' he said, '£2'. I told him I would have it, but that it would have to be delivered to Marlow. This I knew might be difficult owing to petrol rationing, but he said he could do it on his way somewhere else, so we agreed on the price of the carriage, and quite soon afterwards it was delivered from a rather ancient van.

As soon as possible I started to work on one of the small drawers. After a bit I was delighted to find that it had a very superior walnut veneer with a lovely grain, and that it was 'feather-banded'. The method I was using did not disturb the original patina at all and the drawer only needed a good wax polish to make it look as good as it must have done when first made. As it was a lovely summer afternoon I carried drawer after drawer into the garden and went on with my work there, within ear-shot of the shop bell. All the original handles had come off, and large black wooden knobs had taken their place – luckily with small screw-holes, so not much harm had been done to the beautiful drawer fronts, which still bore the impression of the original brass handle-plates. Fortunately, the brass escutcheons were still in place. Reproduction handles were practically unobtainable during the war, but luckily we had recently bought a large drawer full of genuine antique ones from a sale of the contents of a cabinet-maker's business at Henley. I sorted through the drawer and found six matching handles of the right shape and period, and exactly the right size, so that they fitted into the original holes and looked as if they had always been there. This must have been beginner's luck, for it has never happened again, and never will, as alas, there are no more antique handles for sale.

Shortly after this I went over to Henley to see an old dealer friend, from whom we bought and to whom we sold from time to time. There was nothing I wanted, or could afford, in his shop, so he took me into his storeroom at the back to show me an oak piece which had just come in. He was very enthusiastic about it, but my attention was on a pair of chairs which stood nearby. At first sight they appeared to be mahogany, but I had a feeling that the shape was all wrong for that type of wood. I went over to them and had a closer look. The drop-in seats were the originals, although now covered by modern material. The price was quite cheap so I bought them, and he kindly brought them over in his car the next day. I lost no time in getting to work on them. They were walnut, about 1710 in date and looked very beautiful when I had finished them. I then fished out a piece of old Chinese brocade in soft blues and greens from our store of materials and recovered the seats, and the whole effect was highly satisfying. At that

Plate 1 Eighteenth-century French oak table, with boldly carved hoof feet and marble top

Plate 2 (*left*) Long-case clock in walnut and oak by Richard Lee of Great Marlow, 1688; (*right*) slate-topped table

Plate 3   William and Mary walnut table with cross stretcher

Plate 4 (*above*) Prayer book belonging to Edward Venables (personal page to the younger daughters of George III) opened at the service for Gunpowder Treason; (*below*) one of the earliest samplers recorded, worked in bright coloured silks on linen

time of having to pay out coupons for new materials, everyone with forethought in the antique trade bought up bundles of old curtains, etc, from sales. At the sales in big houses there were often very beautiful curtains containing yards of material, that were very well worth buying. Apart from the actual material being useful for chair covers, etc, the linings made good dusters, and the thick interlining excellent polishing cloths. There were also yards and yards of good braid and fringe from the pelmets.

The sequel to this story was that a week later my Henley dealer friend came over to Marlow, and asked if I had any walnut for him. Grinning to myself I replied that I had a beautiful pair of walnut chairs upstairs, and led him up to our drawing-room, where the chairs stood on either side of a card table. His face lit up. 'That's a nice pair of chairs,' he said, then, as he got nearer, 'but surely I've seen them somewhere before?' 'You have,' I answered, 'you sold them to me as mahogany last week.' He clapped me happily on the back, and said thoughtfully as he followed me downstairs, 'now why couldn't *I* have done that?' The answer to his question was I think that, like a great many other people in the trade at that time he only looked at things superficially, going more by the colour of the wood than by the shape. Anyone really interested in discovering disguised antique furniture should get well acquainted with the shapes of each period. This is not difficult to do. There are a great many well-illustrated books on antique furniture in most libraries, that can be taken out and studied, and will prove a great help.

To quote another case showing how a knowledge of shape helps. Some years ago we bought a dressing-stool from a well-known country dealer. It was standing outside his shop, and caught our attention because of its cabriole legs and graceful pad feet. We were on the opposite side of a busy road, and had to wait some time before the traffic cleared enough for us to cross over, so we could see that the seat which had a chintz loose-cover was generous in size. When we reached it, we found that the legs were stained with a dark mahogany varnish but, on turning it up, we found that the feet showed signs of considerable wear, so we bought it. The assistant informed us, as he was wrapping it up, that it was going cheap because it was only reproduction mahogany. We took it back with us in the car, and immediately removed the canvas underneath the seat that had been put on to conceal the webbing, etc. We discovered then that the framework was of early eighteenth-century construction and, judging by the enormous number of tack-holes in it, a great many different coverings had been on the seat since the time of its manufacture. There was not much trouble in removing the varnish from the legs, which proved to be of honey-coloured apple wood; and we were well pleased with our bargain.

Sometimes one has practically nothing to go on but the shape of a piece, as was the case once with a wing armchair, on which varnish and covering had combined effectively to disguise its antiquity. We saw it just after the war in the window of a large furniture shop in High Wycombe (long since demolished) which sold new, second-hand and antique furniture. One must realise that during the war, and for some little time afterwards, the making of modern furniture was considerably constricted owing to the very small amount of seasoned wood which was allowed to the manufacturers. Modern furniture shops were therefore not able to buy anywhere near enough new furniture to fill their windows and showrooms. So they bought instead, either privately or at sales, good second-hand furniture, which they then had done up to look like new. If, as very often happened, some of it was antique, it made no difference to them, and it was all done up likewise. Hence all antique dealers spent a great deal of time prowling about modern furniture shops to find stock for themselves, and were very well rewarded. Indeed most of us felt quite sad when the full quota of seasoned timber was at last restored to the modern furniture manufacturer, and modern furniture shops had no further need of buying 'second-hand'. The chair we saw in the window of this High Wycombe shop was so beautifully done up that it almost made us believe it was quite new. But the graceful shape of the wings and arms was too good to be a cheap modern edition, so we bought it. Denuded of its striped silk Regency cover, the carefully hidden secret was immediately discovered. The inner canvas and horsehair stuffing were early Georgian. It just remained for us to clean the mahogany stain and French polish from the legs, to find that they were walnut. We had at the time no material 'put by' sufficiently good to cover it, so sold it in its uncovered state to the trade.

About six months later we called on some friends who had a shop about twelve miles distant, and were taken with pride to look at a wonderful early wing armchair which had just been returned from a high-class antique upholsterers. I had an idea of what we were going to see, on our way to the showroom, and I was right. There, in all the pride and glory of a really beautiful covering, stood our erstwhile modern chair! We did not say anything, how could we, especially when we knew that our host made a habit of visiting the shop the chair had originally come from, at least twice a week. Had the chair been sold to the ordinary furniture buyer its secret would probably never have been discovered, and it would have ended up as so many antiques do, on a rubbish dump. It makes one wonder how many such pieces have come to this inglorious end, and how much beautiful furniture has been lost to the world in this manner.

Shape we have agreed is important; but occasionally something turns up of a shape not very familiar to us and which might perplex if we merely heard about it, and were not in a position to see and handle it. Something of this sort happened to me once in the days when sets of wheel-back chairs were quite easy to obtain. It was a very wet winter's day and a man drew up in his car and came in to ask if I would like to buy a wheel-back chair. I said that there was not much sale for single wheel-back chairs and I did not think I should be interested in seeing his. 'Ah,' he replied, 'but this really has a "wheel" back.' And to my astonishment when he brought it in, the back of the chair was a finely turned wooden wheel just flattened where the spokes fitted into the seat. It was nearly black in colour, and it struck me that it would look extremely well with a seventeenth-century Scottish spinning wheel we had in our own room; so I paid him what he asked for it. For some months I dusted that chair every day. Spring came, and as the sun got stronger it shone on the chair, and one day I noticed a reddish gleam on one of the spokes. I took it to the window and discovered more reddish gleams. I scratched a little bit at the back of one of them, and found the black – which I had taken to be the original dark finish often used on beech chairs – was in fact a black varnish. Because it was a good-quality Victorian varnish, this took a long time to remove, but the end was worth it. My wheel-back chair was made of yew-tree, and is the only one of its kind I have ever seen!

There were several kinds of Victorian varnish. One of them gave a finish to furniture similar to that found on the frames of pianos. It very completely disguised an early Georgian sideboard with cabriole legs that was standing outside a second-hand shop in a neighbouring town, and I passed it on the bus several times before I realised it could not, in fact, be a reproduction. So I alighted from the bus and went and examined it. The handles were genuine antiques, the inside of the drawers proved that they were too, and the back was certainly not modern. The varnish was of the unchippable variety and I was not sure I could deal with it, but the sideboard was very cheap, and I felt I had to have it. My husband was in the army at the time, so the carpenter and I spent hours and hours and hours, getting the varnish off the wood the hard way, without using any solvents at all. As soon as we had finished one drawer front, we found it to be of fruit wood and a lovely golden brown. There was no worm in the piece, and no repairs had ever been done to it. I eventually sold it to a dealer who visited the shop regularly every week.

About three weeks later my husband came home on leave, and suggested we should go to the Cotswolds for the day. This we did, and went to see a fascinating shop at Stow-on-the-Wold (now long gone – but never to be forgotten)! It was kept by a really charming old lady with a profound knowledge of Queen Anne bedspreads and fabrics, and antique furniture. There, to my amusement, I found my sideboard standing in the place of honour. The price was about ten times more than I had given for it. My husband was drawn towards it as steel to a magnet, but I walked round a corner, and was much edified to hear it described as a beautiful eighteenth-century piece in entirely untouched condition! I did not blame her; how could she know of the hours I had spent in ensuring that this would be so. I knew my husband was tempted, but I shook my head at him. When finally we left the shop, having made other purchases, I explained that I could not bear to pay ten times more than the original price I had given for a piece which I had discovered, and on which I had spent so much time. There was no doubt at all that it was really worth all she was asking for it, but I thought somebody else should have a chance of buying it. And I was glad to find that – somewhat reluctantly – my husband was inclined to agree with me!

Removing Varnish, or Cheap French Polish
Varnish

If this chips off easily it is not really necessary to remove it with stripper, just scrape it off with the edge of a copper coin. The coin should be held at an angle. Do not press too hard, especially on soft woods. It may be a bit arm-aching, but it is far the best way of doing it. For one reason it does not disturb the patina, and polish of the wood underneath, and it will only need an ordinary polish afterwards. Another reason is that all the mess, inconvenience and danger of strippers is avoided. Also it is a supremely fascinating job, and everybody will want to have a go. Do not let them, especially if they are heavy-handed. This applies to any method of stripping. One person only, if possible, should start and finish the job. No two people work in the same way – and it will show!

French Polish

I was taught when training always to take off an unwanted finish with the same medium that had been used to put it on. French polish is, or was, put on with methylated spirit; therefore methylated spirit will remove it. But before rushing for the 'meths', let me offer a word or two of advice. Cheap French polish will come off easily when rubbed with this agent and a little fine wire wool. But if it is a mahogany piece you are dealing with, have a care. This method may sound easy, but I can assure you that it is not. There are all kinds of pitfalls lying in wait for the amateur; for instance you must know exactly when to stop, or you will find that you have not only removed the top layer of French polish but the original shellac one underneath it as well and, if the piece is a good antique, you will have damaged it. It would be better to have the work done by a cabinet-worker who is an expert in dealing with antique furniture.

Another pitfall lies ahead for the unwary. If you are removing a dark-stain French polish from a piece made of light wood and wondering why it had ever been applied, you will soon find out, when you discover a patch or mend has been effected with a dark piece of wood, usually in a conspicuous place. A dark varnish stain was then applied to the whole piece to cover up the discrepancy. Alas! it is now only too glaringly apparent, and you are faced with the problem of either having to bleach the patch, or restain the article. And only an expert can help you here.

Using a Stripper

When it is necessary for any reason to apply a stripper, read all the instructions carefully on the bottle before you open it. It is better, if possible, to carry out the whole operation out-of-doors, for the smell is very strong, all-pervading, and overpowering if used in a small room. Before beginning the operation at all, collect everything you may want for it: newspapers, rags, meths, stripper and the receptacle you put it in, sandpaper, knives, brushes and swabs, and have them close at hand. Keep everything well away from young children and animals, and cover your clothing, with an old raincoat or something similar, and your hands with rubber gloves. Do not forget it is an acid you are using, and that acid burns are very painful. The antidote is cold water, quickly applied.

On country furniture made of oak, beech, ash, chestnut, etc, that has suffered years of dirt and ill treatment as well as varnish, apply the stripper liberally with a soft paint-brush or cotton mop, leave it alone for about ten minutes to do its work, then wipe the resultant mess away with soft rags. Do not be too impatient, or try to hasten the process by scraping with knives or abrasives. The scraping noise is an unnecessary annoyance and in the end you will only have to apply another coat all over again, thus wasting time and stripper. When you have finished your job, put brushes, mops, etc, in a jar of water, and rinse out the receptacle from which stripper was used. The piece should then be washed down with methylated spirit and a wax polish applied. This is all the better for being left on for a few hours before the final polish is given.

When stripping varnish from fine woods such as walnut, yew-tree or fruit wood, apply the stripper sparingly with a soft brush. Do a small section at a time, and rub wax in well before proceeding with the next section.

When transferring stripper from the bottle to the container you intend to use – a large saucer is best – never put it into a plastic container. It will quickly burn a hole in the bottom, and you will not only lose the stripper, but find other surfaces have been damaged by it. Never use caustic soda on any wood but pine or deal, and not even then unless there is no other alternative.

Wax Polishing

As this is essential after any form of stripping, I offer the following advice. Alway use a wax polish, never a silicon, on antiques. There is a good one with a beeswax base on the market. It was formerly made and sold by an old cabinet-maker in Kent, who would supply it to us in any kind of tin that came to hand. He finally sold the recipe to a well-known London firm, and it is now packed in uniform blue tins and sold by all big stores, and many antique shops. There is also a purely vegetable white wax, which seems expensive at £1 for a very small tin. But one needs so very little to get a most beautiful polish, that it is both economical and highly valuable for small objects of treen, papier-mâché, gilded wood, lacquer, etc; and it has the property also of being well-nigh finger-print proof. For applying wax of any kind, use soft woollen cloths, or soft brushes. Do not use a white polish on a dark wood, especially if it is a carved piece, as it gets into the cracks and hardens there, which makes it difficult to remove.

If a large flat surface needs a heavy polish, wrap a heavy object, such as a brick or an old-fashioned flat-iron in a thick layer of flannel or old blanket, and press down on it hard when polishing. These are old-fashioned devices, but in my experience they are often the best.

Keep your polishing dusters clean, and boil them frequently, especially after use with a dark polish. One final word, a warm duster will give a better polish than a cold one.

3 Antiques Disguised by Paint or Dirt

Before immersing ourselves too deeply in the problems connected with furniture and other antiques disguised in this way, we ought to try and find out the reasons for using paint at all. By doing so we shall discover the proper way of dealing with it.

Paint Used as a Decoration

From very early times paint was used as a decoration for walls as well as furniture. Plaster walls in the houses of the rich were painted with allegorical, historical or religious scenes, and artists were paid large sums for their work. Very little of this decoration survives today, partly because other forms of decoration superseded these murals. The walls of the houses of the less rich were treated differently. Most medieval houses had low ceilings and small windows, and were therefore dark. Painted murals were an expensive form of decoration, but those who could afford to do so hung bright materials on their walls, or tapestries woven or embroidered in bright colours. These were removable. They could be taken from room to room if required, or if the owners removed to another house.

In Scandinavian countries a great deal of the furniture has always been painted, and not only the furniture but household implements as well – pails, mangling boards, washing bats, etc. This form of gay and bright decoration is, strangely enough, almost identical with that used on barges in England. Here brightly decorated kettles, tubs, water-carriers, etc, were, and still are, used by bargees, and such things are now being widely collected. No one would dream of stripping off this sort of decoration because the object so decorated would be quite uninteresting without it.

In the Middle Ages if murals were not used by the rich, the furniture was painted instead. This was especially the case where large cupboards were concerned. The doors and panels, being made of wood which very often had little basic attraction by itself, were painted with full-length pictures of saints and scripture subjects, while the panels of chests were painted with smaller subjects, and this practice continued right up to the end of the sixteenth century at least. One of our most interesting discoveries was of a sixteenth-century chest, with Elizabethan emblems painted on the three front panels. One bore the royal coat-of-arms of the Tudors (incorporating the Welsh dragon instead of the Scottish unicorn) while the other two were embellished with Tudor roses, angels, the letters E.R. and curious objects – very popular in the needlework of the time – such as caterpillars, bees, etc, and, most interesting of all perhaps, an elephant portrayed with hoofed feet. At this time very few people had actually seen an elephant, and had to fall back on their imaginations when it came to portraying one. (There is a carving of an almost identical elephant on one of the misericords in the choir stalls of Exeter Cathedral.) This chest, a very big one, started life as a dower chest, for it bore the initials of bride and groom in exquisite Elizabethan lettering on the left and right panels. For centuries it had done duty as a grain bin on a farm; we found plenty of evidence of this when we came to clean the interior. Thick dirt disguised the whole piece, and was removed with the greatest possible care in order not to destroy the paintings. The removal disclosed that the framework to the front panels was painted in a chequer pattern of black and white. We left the final cleaning of the painted panels to experts, and it was a magnificent piece when finished. As wood carvers became more proficient, carving succeeded painting as a decoration of oak furniture. Touches of colour and gilding were still used however, to enhance the carvings. This painting of ancient woodwork is referred to as 'polychrome', meaning in plain language 'many colours', and it should only be used in reference to this kind of decoration. But the word 'polychrome' has an attraction, leading to many things being described as 'having their original polychrome' when one coat of ordinary paint has been applied to such things as Windsor chairs!

Painting as a form of decoration for furniture was revived again in the eighteenth century. Some Sheraton and Hepplewhite furniture was painted all over. The paint was mainly pastel coloured, and parts of the piece were gilded. Some mahogany and satinwood furniture was painted with garlands of flowers and other designs. There was also at this time a craze for furniture made of imitation bamboo, painted in yellows and browns. Later, in Regency days when brass-decorated rosewood furniture was fashionable, beech was painted to simulate rosewood. Age, usage and continual cleaning have all combined to remove a great deal of the original decoration from all these species of painted furniture. They look shabby – so what can be done with them? There are artists specially trained who will repaint pieces so damaged, but it is an expensive process. Some of us may think we can do it ourselves, but the kind of paint being manufactured today is not of the same quality, composition or range of colour as it was 200 years ago, and 'do-it-yourself' painted furniture will be a disappointment, and in any case cannot be said to be in 'the original condition'. Stripped and polished, it still retains the antique look, but the value is considerably lowered, so the question of finish remains a vexed one.

Oak-graining

There is yet another painted finish – that of imitation oak-graining which was achieved by painting the wood a light tan colour and, when dry, applying a darker colour which, before becoming quite dry, was partially wiped away in such a manner as to suggest the graining of oak. This was looked upon in Edwardian days as a typical Victorian invention for getting an oak effect without having to pay the full price for it; consequently 'graining' became almost a dirty word. But lately much more has been found out about it. To begin with it goes back for centuries. It was, however, perhaps a money-saver for builders who could not afford to pay for oak, which was always in demand in certain quarters for shipbuilding. A substitute wood was used for outer doors and window frames, and this was then 'grained' to give an oak appearance. I have watched the operation, and it is absolutely fascinating – and in itself an art. This graining process was done on furniture in Scotland where there was a natural scarcity of oak, but a good supply of pine. *Early* examples of furniture painted in this way do not often turn up in England, and probably would not be recognised for what they were if they did.

Not long ago we were touring in Norfolk (where magnificent oak forests still abound) when we spied a very likely looking antique shop. It was early closing day in that part of the world so the shop was shut. We studied the stock through the windows, and spied in the back of the shop a small early desk-on-stand in oak. We liked the look of it very much, and returned next day to examine it more closely, which resulted in our buying it. Arrived home we stocked it, priced it, and put it in the showroom that contained our early pieces. When I went to polish it I noticed that the front of one of the small drawers was not of oak but of grained pine, which led me to examine the whole piece in a strong light. To my surprise I found that it was all of early pine very delicately grained, and which had acquired through years of wear and polish, a very fine patina. It was a seventeenth-century piece made when there was plenty of oak in England. Therefore, the presumption was that it had been brought from Scotland.

It had been sold to us as oak, and we had bought it as such, because up to that time we had never seen any early 'grained' *furniture* before. Since then I have seen a Jacobean chest-of-drawers (in the north of England) and later we bought from Scotland an early swinging-cradle in stripped pine, on which in various places were traces of graining. It is true that in untouched condition these 'grained' pine pieces are more valuable than the oak equivalents, on account of their rarity.

Paint Used as a Preservative

Before iron garden furniture was introduced in the early nineteenth century, stick-back Windsor chairs were used out-of-doors, both in gardens and in the London parks. They were made of beech, painted white to preserve the wood. Single chairs, armchairs and stick-back settles were made for gardens. These stick-back chairs were also popular in inns and eating houses, usually painted green or red. Settles of ash, oak and elm were also painted – as were cricket tables (only the legs, as a rule, the tops were kept scrubbed). Stick-back chairs are now very popular for use with gate-leg tables, but the demand for sets of six is almost impossible to meet. People are now making up Harlequin sets for themselves. Occasionally these painted chairs turn up, with the paint worn off completely in the places which get the most wear – the seat, front 'sticks', arms, front legs, etc. But it still remains thick on the back, sides of seat, and on the back and sides of the sticks. As beech is a nicely grained wood which takes a high polish, this is obviously a case where stripping will add to the value and beauty of the chairs.

When Stripping is Advisable

Other clear cases for stripping are where, through sheer ignorance, paint has been applied to furniture in recent times; such as a dresser we once bought, which had been painted bright yellow! It was a very fine early eighteenth-century dresser with a plate-rack, three drawers and a pot-board, the legs were sturdy and had chamfered sides, and the lines of the whole piece very satisfying. Groaning at the thought that all this yellow paint would have to be removed, we chipped a bit off. We groaned still more when we found there were four more coats underneath it – blue, brown, red and white. But it was a fine piece, and looked splendid when restored to its original condition.

There was also the long-case clock we went to see. This had been painted red by evacuees during World War II who had also mounted it on another base about 18in high, in order that a longer rope could be used to carry the weight. The dial was covered with thick white bath enamel and, of course, it was not in working order. The poor thing looked quite desperate. But there were spiral pillars at each side of the face underneath a flat hood, and the clock looked much too narrow for its height. Having bought it I cleaned a bit of the dial and found the name and date, Richard Lee of Great Marlow 1688 – his name is in the *Directory of Clock Makers*. At the same time my husband had discovered that the door to the case was walnut under the red paint. We sent the case to the cabinet-maker, the dial to a specialist on the subject and the clock to the clock-mender, and when it returned it was quite unrecognisable. The case was of oak and walnut, the face of brass and silver-gilt and the clock had only needed a clean and a new rope to put it into going order. We decided to keep it for ourselves. Here stripping had been the only thing to do, but we knew it should be done by experts as obviously it was a valuable piece (Plate 2).

Some readers may want to know about furniture made of pine. Should it be stripped? This is purely a matter of personal taste. Pine was used quite extensively in the nineteenth century for painted furniture such as bedroom suites for secondary rooms, comprising dressing-table, washing-stand, chest-of-drawers and a wardrobe – 'gentleman's' variety. It was usually painted a drab yellow with brown lines round the edges. The knobs were of white china, and the feet of the type known as 'Victorian onions'. During World War II this kind of furniture was bought up in quantity by one of the large stores with an 'antique' department, and redecorated in daintier colours. The feet were changed for eighteenth-century-type 'bracket' feet, and 'Georgian' brass knobs were screwed on in the place of the white china ones. It sold readily in the 'antique' department. Now, after some thirty or forty years' wear, the pieces have grown shabby and have reverted to their former cheap price. They must either be repainted or stripped, and stripping is a smarter and cheaper finish for these 'near' antiques.

Pine dressers and cupboards were kitchen fitments in Victorian days. These were painted – usually stone colour. The dresser working-top though was made of a slab of thick oak and left unpainted as it was expected it would need scrubbing. When Victorian houses are pulled down, these dressers come on the market again, carefully stripped and finished, and are in great demand. Pine was often used in conjunction with oak for the construction of refectory-type tables used in farm-house kitchens and dairies, and the kitchens of large houses in the eighteenth century. These were always kept scrubbed.

Another use for pine was to make the carcases of walnut-veneered or lacquered furniture, in the late seventeenth and early eighteenth centuries. The reason for this was that it was a soft wood on which veneers would stick tightly, and not fly off as they did on harder wood such as oak. A piece of walnut furniture that has lost some of its veneer can always be restored by an expert cabinet-maker, missing pieces of veneer being replaced by antique veneering, so that the piece when finished will look as good as new. This is not the case, however, with lacquered furniture which is much more vulnerable to scratches, knocks and damp. Through the ages chunks of lacquer will have fallen off with no expert to replace them, so at length, in order to match the missing piece and look more respectable, the whole of the lacquer will have been removed and the corner cupboard or long-case clock stained or painted – these were favourite pieces of furniture for lacquering. Other pieces of lacquered furniture have suffered in this way too. In a tiny antique shop in Dorset some years ago we came upon a piece of stripped pine furniture that seemed to us to be unique. It was a corner bureau book-case. This at one time quite obviously had been lacquered, probably red. The original hinges were still there, and they were the pierced butterfly variety which were customary on such a piece. The pine was of the plain smooth kind which takes a beautiful mellow honey-colour when polished. When we asked the price we were told, 'Oh! that was a great disappointment to us, it was painted red, and we thought it was walnut underneath, but it was only pine, we'd be glad to get rid of it!' They did get rid of it, to us, and when we had finished polishing it looked really lovely, and was bought almost immediately.

Any stripped pine cupboards that have bow fronts, are almost sure to have been lacquered. Usually the bow is very pronounced, the shelves prettily shaped inside, and on the flat top is an extension, right at the back, in the form of two or three open shelves with curved sides narrowing in width until they end in a point. We have one in our office at the shop, to house special tea-things and glasses for use when entertaining our friends. The wood has now achieved a polish like amber both in colour and to touch. Everyone immediately wants to buy it; but it is not for sale. My own opinion is that a Queen Anne bow-fronted cupboard of pine is worth more than an oak one. It is earlier in period and much more interesting in appearance. A friend bought one not long ago which had been stained to look like oak and had the original butterfly hinges. On our advice he had it stripped and polished, and was delighted with it.

Removing Paint

In the days before stripping agents appeared on the market, the universal method of stripping off paint was by scrubbing it with a strong solution of 'Manger's Sugar Soap' in nearly boiling water. Therefore, anything too big to go into the kitchen sink was too messy a job to do anywhere but out-of-doors, and even then it made a mess of the yard. It was necessary to do it in a place where the water could run away easily, and within easy reach of a boiling kettle.

The dresser I mentioned just now that had five coats of paint on it was therefore a problem. A painter had left his blow-lamp behind, and my husband decided he would burn the paint off the plate-rack with that. This, I hasten to say, is not a wise thing to use on anything antique (including the paint on woodwork in old buildings). Apart from the danger of fire, there is a danger of scorching the furniture. If not a blow-lamp – then what? A sudden inspiration decided me to use gentler means, and I can recommend this method to anyone who does not want to use a stripping agent.

Two ordinary old-fashioned flat-irons will be needed, heated one after the other on a boiling-plate or gas ring. Also a good thick iron-holder, and a broad stripping knife. The method is simplicity itself. As soon as the iron has attained a good heat, just iron the surface to be stripped, holding the iron in the left hand and following it along with the stripping knife in the right. Do this until the iron cools, scrape off any paint adhering to the latter's surface, replace on the ring, and in its place use the fresh iron which has been heating. This is a fascinating occupation. All the paint comes off with one 'iron' – all five in our case! It curls up into little dry rings, which are easy to sweep up; the smell is not unpleasant, and the operation reasonably quick. If a dresser has to be stripped, do the top of the base first and the pot-board, if there is one, then turn it on its back and do the front, and the fronts of all the legs. Turn it upright again to do the sides, which will not be difficult to do as long as a tight grip is kept on the iron to prevent it slipping over. This operation sounds absurdly amateurish, and can only be done on flat surfaces, but it does save a lot of mess. Any paint that remains in crevices, etc, can be gouged out with a hot metal skewer. After the ironing operation is over, wash the piece down carefully, either with a little sugar soap, or with a cloth dipped in turpentine, to remove any bits of paint left here and there. When dry, finish with a couple of wax polishings.

In the case of removing a top coat only, without injuring the original painting underneath, just soften the paint with an application of linseed oil, then scrape the top layer away bit by bit with a blunt penknife. This is a long and tiring business, as it all has to be done very gently. Start on a place that has been damaged – this will be easier to work from as some of the paint will have been removed. Bits of paint left here and there can be eradicated by rubbing gently with a cloth dipped in turpentine. Do not try to do too much at a time.

Stripping Paint from Stick-back Chairs

Using a good stripper, apply it to the chair a little at a time, leave it for a while to do its work of loosening the paint and then remove it with the aid of superfine wire wool, a blunt penknife, or just simply with old rags. As the paint is removed, cover the place with polish, and continue until finished. Because much of the wood has been exposed where the original paint has worn off, it will have achieved a slightly darker colour than that from which the paint has just been stripped. Cover the latter with a darker wax, rubbing it well in, and leaving it for several hours before polishing. A soft boot-brush is often a great help when polishing spindles.

Colour Matching Gate-leg Tables

Sometimes painted dressers and oak gate-leg tables that have been in use on farms, have had the working-tops scrubbed. This is all right where a painted dresser is going to be stripped entirely; but one usually does not strip the ancient original colouring matter from the turned legs of a gate-leg table. Getting the almost white table top up to the colour of the legs is a very tricky job, and should never be attempted by an amateur. It should be handed over to a cabinet-maker well versed in the treatment of antique furniture – he will know exactly what to do, and how to do it, and the job need not necessarily be long or expensive.

Removing Dirt

By this I mean real surface dirt, and not years of patina which must not be removed. It congregates just where one would expect: on the backs of settles and high Windsor chairs, where innumerable greasy heads have rested; between, and at the base of the 'sticks' on these chairs; and, of course, on the bottoms of the legs – as it does on any piece of furniture. There is another sort of greasy dirt which collects on the lower shelves of dressers. Sometimes really thick deposits of this dirt can be scraped off with a blunt knife. Keep the polishing wax handy, and rub it in as soon as the dirt has been removed.

A very slight application of stripper will quickly remove dirt. It should be put on and almost immediately wiped off again with soft pieces of rag. There is also a liquid cleaner on the market, put out by the same firm which supplies the wax polish. This, however, will not remove long-standing dirt. There are also one or two old and trusted recipes which will be found at the end of this book.

Plate 5   (*above*) A 'dressed' needlework picture. The dresses worn by the ladies are of actual materials, the folds, etc, being indicated by 'outline' stitch; (*below*) felt appliqué picture combined with needlework, of boy and girl

Plate 6   Pair of pictures in felt appliqué work by Smart, the tailor of Frant, Sussex: (*above*) 'Betty the Goosewoman'; (*below*) 'Dick the Postman'

Plate 7 An 'in memoriam' picture in superb hair work, with gilt and pearl
additions, in original frame

Plate 8 (*left*) Spanish or Portuguese chasuble in which the late seventeenth-century needlework has been re-attached to another material about 200 years later. The faces of the angels are of solid silver; (*right*) pole screen in papier-mâché. An exceptionally fine piece. The picture was probably painted by Landseer, who was said to do such work as 'pot-boilers'

It is astonishing how much dirt can disguise a lovely piece of furniture. The slate-topped table in Plate 2 is a very good instance of this. I bought it, thinking that the top alone was painted. This had been kept clean, and only needed a polish. The base appeared to be of black japanned wood, or wood with a thin layer of papier-mâché applied; but it had an unpleasantly rough coating of dirt on it which deadened the lacquer. This I started to remove with a dampened soapy flannel, working from the top of the stem downward. Towards the bottom I was surprised to see some painted flowers appearing. When I reached the base, more flowers – beautifully painted – appeared. Little sprigs of them were even painted on the three feet. I dried it carefully, and started all over again, this time with liquid white polish. After a little gentle rubbing with this, the whole charming decoration came to light.

The second example of dirt – this time disguising the wood – was a table I once bought in a second-hand shop. It was a William and Mary period table, with a drawer, turned legs and a cross stretcher (Plate 3). There was at least a quarter of an inch of combined solid dirt and grease all over it. Although on the price ticket the table was described as oak, I was convinced it was walnut, and as soon as possible started cleaning operations. I began with the top, which turned out to be feather-banded walnut veneered on oak. The drawer was also walnut, with oak mouldings. The stretcher was solid walnut, and so were the turned legs and burr feet. Having spent a lot of time and energy cleaning it I refused to put it in the shop. And it is at home in the same room as the long-case oak and walnut clock.

Both these beautiful pieces are examples of treasures completely disguised by paint or dirt. But the shape of both was the clue to making such exciting discoveries, which delight me every time I look at them. The cost of the two together was less than £50; therefore the amount of profit I could make would be considerable. But I am not tempted to sell them – apart from their beauty and the joy I get from them, they hold so many happy memories that to sell them would be like getting rid of old friends.

Some time after writing this chapter I was delighted to come across the following passage in Alan Jolson's *Under a Suffolk Sky*. He is writing about a cooking implement called a 'salamander' (a long iron bar with a flat circular end) which was heated in the fire and then held over milk puddings, etc, to brown them, and adds:

This iron by the way, was also used by house-painters in the burning off of old paint, before the blow-lamp was invented. A boy held the heated iron near the paint while the man scraped off the old stain under its heat.

So, if no flat-irons are obtainable one can always make do with a salamander.

4 Needlework and Fabrics Disguised by Bad Framing, Dirt or Age

Samplers

Stitch Samplers

I am convinced, from my own experience, that many early and important samplers have been thrown away or destroyed, simply because they were not recognised for what they were. I have stressed the need for the knowledge of the shapes of furniture, in order to recognise a good piece under a heavy disguise of dirt, paint or varnish. The same thing can be said about early samplers disguised by dirt or bad framing – they can be easily recognised by their shape.

Samplers worked by little girls in the late seventeenth and early eighteenth centuries were the outcome of the Jacobean silk embroidery done by their mothers on the ends of linen towels, pillow cases, etc. Those ladies knew that several stitches would be embodied in their work. To refresh their memories they embroidered a sample of each different stitch worked into a pattern on narrow strips of canvas or linen that could be rolled up and kept in the workbasket, and referred to as needed. Their friends and female relations, perhaps knew different kinds of stitches and patterns; these they exchanged with each other, embroidering each fresh stitch on their 'sempler' or 'sampler'. I have recently had the great good luck to acquire privately a very early stitch sampler of this kind (Plate 4). It is worked in silk on linen, and six different designs are shown half worked. I give them in detail here because they are extremely interesting.

Design no 1 is a diamond. On the extreme left is a strawberry, on top a flower that could be a clover, on the right a carnation, and at the bottom a pomegranate. These are worked in different colours on a green background.

Design no 2 is a narrow strip. An S-shaped line divides a strawberry or raspberry from a simple white four-petalled flower, the background yellow.

Design no 3 is an X in green and gold, over a square containing a Tudor rose worked in red with a gold centre.

Design no 4 is an ornate carnation with leaves worked in pink and green in a green border Below to the right is a yellow buttercup with leaves.

Design no 5 is an acorn with oak leaves in green, on a pink background, with a border of cubes in two shades of blue, at each corner is a gold cross.

Design no 6 is a diamond shape containing a simple pink Tudor rose on a green background, surrounded by four-petalled flowers on a gold surrounding bar, with blue back-to-back triangles.

There is very faint evidence to the right of the date that the design was finely drawn in a pale red colour. In the bottom left-hand corner the letters 's.l. 1640' are worked in green. The front of this sampler is much faded, but the colour at the back is as good as new, and gives a perfect idea of how bright and glowing the colours were. Also the faint 'pattern' lines are more easily seen. For these reasons the sampler will be framed between two pieces of glass, so that nothing of this outstanding early sampler should be lost.

When a girl reached the age of seven or eight she was instructed how to work as many of these stiches as possible in one piece of needlework, called a 'sampler'. I think that probably the idea behind this working of a sampler was to carry on into the girl's further education not only a knowledge of stitchery but the lessons she had already learned, almost as a baby, from the horn books she had carried suspended on a ribbon from her waist. Horn books contained the alphabet, numerals up to ten, and very often the Lord's Prayer, and these were all worked by the child on narrow pieces of fine linen or canvas, like her mother's sampler. And so we find the alphabet in about three different methods of stitching; numerals done in the same way, interspersed between bands of astonishingly fine stitchery; texts, mainly from the Old Testament, were also incorporated, especially those inveighing against vanity or idleness. At the end (or more rarely the beginning) of this piece of work, the child also embroidered her name, and the date on which the piece was finished. It was then rolled up and put away. These narrow samplers were made well into the eighteenth century. The later ones incorporated verses (thought out by the governess?) in which the virtues of the girl's parents were extolled, and her own indebtedness to them expressed.

Towards the middle of the eighteenth century, when samplers became entirely children's work, the shape of the samplers changed, and became shorter and wider. The subjects also changed. Instead of rows of ornate stitchery, figures appeared and houses, churches, castles, ships, and all kinds of animals and birds, as well as insects. A delightfully naïve representation of Adam and Eve on either side of the tree of Life, round which the serpent was twined, was a favourite subject. Sometimes a verse of a hymn, or a secular verse (though still pious). Rows of different initials, representing each member of the family were also incorporated.

But to return to the early samplers. As these had never been displayed, they were never framed until the end of the nineteenth century, when there was a sentimental addiction to such things. Their frames, therefore, are those of the late Victorian or Edwardian period – often versions of black and gilt 'Hogarth' frames. But as the taste then was for the later more colourful sampler, more often than not these narrow samplers were not thought much of, and the frames are not only cheap but the framing has obviously been done by amateurs, with no idea of what to do to keep the dust out. So the glass is badly fitted, the 'backing paper' (a bit of an old piece of wrapping paper) has split, and let in both moth and woodworm. And the framed sampler is hanging up in a dark corner of a shop, the glass so dirty it almost conceals the needlework, and because there is no 'picture' or a gilt frame, the ordinary antique buyer takes no notice of it. And this is where anyone with a knowledge of shape will score, for these early samplers are far more valuable than the later, well-framed pretty ones.

As these early samplers were worked on a very fine unbleached linen or canvas neatly hemstitched round the edge, framing presents a problem. Great care must be taken not to obscure the edge of the work by the frame, it is better to have it mounted on something which extends about $\frac{1}{4}$in all round. A very narrow unobtrusive gilt frame is the most successful way of showing off the needlework.

It is as well to make a 'translation' of the words, and keep it with the sampler. A text of the whole wording must have been made for the child to copy, but very young children could not understand the very long words used and copied the text blindly. This has been quite evident in several I have had. Capitals have been used indiscriminately; half a word has been left on one line, and after about an inch and a half of embroidery, is continued on the first line of writing after that; full stops and commas are either left out altogether, or dotted about haphazardly. Even if the child did understand, her spelling sometimes slipped up. I remember seeing one of these samplers on which the whole of the Ten Commandments had been laboriously worked. When it came to the tenth commandment she had embroidered, with unconscious humour, 'Thou shalt not covet thy neighbour's wife, nor his servant, nor his maid, nor his ox, nor his arse, nor anything that is his!'

The later eighteenth- and early nineteenth-century samplers were often worked by girls in their last year at school, and I have had evidence that they were framed by a local frame-maker, so that the whole thing could be taken home in a finished condition to show off their prowess to their parents. The frames were Georgian gilt ones, some of them quite handsome. The sampler was first tacked all the way round the edge of a narrow wooden stretcher. This was secured in the frame with brads, and a piece of thick paper pasted over the back to prevent dust or moth from getting in through the cracks. Always examine this paper carefully if original. It may have the name of the girl who worked the sampler written on the back, together with other interesting details; or the trade-plate of the frame-maker may be pasted on it, thus giving an extra cachet to the frame.

We rarely buy samplers worked after 1830 unless they come from Scotland, when we will go up to 1840. Scottish samplers have always a tremendous amount of interesting family detail on them, but they are worked in much more sombre colours, almost as if it were wrong to use anything bright. They usually incorporate a lot of worked crowns and coronets, and are much bigger than the English variety. They are framed in dark heavy frames of walnut, rosewood, mahogany, or painted pine. They are not always the work of children. One we had was worked by a young bride, and gave the name of her husband and the initials of many members of the family on both sides. Those who had departed this life (presumably) being worked in black!

'Darning' Samplers

Another kind of sampler which might easily be left behind as uninteresting, is the 'darning' sampler. This was the way the girl was taught to do superfine darning on linen or muslin. On a 12in square of gauze, four or five different kinds of darning were done in different coloured very fine silks. This darning really mended the holes which had been purposely cut in the material, and are miraculous pieces of fine needlework. There is usually a wreath of different coloured flowers encircling the darns; this is done in ordinary embroidery. The girl's name, and the date, are worked at the bottom in very small fine lettering. In some cases this is done in human hair. Occasionally, the holes were not cut. I have just acquired one where the darns were done over a square inch of the material without stitching it. If this kind of sampler is in an uninteresting frame, and with a dusty glass, it would be quite an easy thing to overlook it. But they are really very rare, and much sought after by collectors.

Maps

There are two main kinds of these; both were taught at girls' finishing schools. The prettier of the two, and the most eye-catching, was oval, worked in different coloured silks on a cream satin background. Round the edge was worked a wreath of different coloured flowers, and the map was framed in a fairly wide gold frame. In the eighteenth century there was a girls' finishing school in St Peter's

Street in Marlow (then known as Duck Lane, from the fact that there used to be a 'ducking stool' at the river end). At this school this kind of map was a speciality. And they often used to turn up at sales in the large houses in the district when we lived there some years ago. The schoolhouse, now known as The Fisherman's Retreat, is still standing.

The other kind of map was worked in tambour stitch on a fine oblong gauze background. The girl's name, and often that of the school, was worked in a very fine black silk somewhere on the canvas, and in the top right-hand corner was a picture of Britannia with a man-of-war in the background, worked in different coloured silks. The frame to this was of heavy gilt, usually with a black glass inset, decorated with gold. These maps on gauze backgrounds have usually worn better than those worked on satin. The latter material is inclined to split.

First-aid for Distressed Samplers

The first thing to do with a dirty-looking sampler it to take it out of the frame. It will be surprising how much cleaner it will immediately appear once it is away from its mucky surroundings. If the frame is not the original and appears unsuitable, throw it away. Now place the sampler on a clean piece of white paper, and rub very gently with breadcrumbs on both sides. I find the best kind of bread to use is a roll, torn apart. Do not let the crust touch the material, or it may drag at the threads. As the bread gets dirty, take a fresh piece, until the whole sampler is as clean as possible. Never wash samplers, more have been ruined by this treatment than by any other cause. Then place the sampler carefully between two sheets of clean white paper and put it under a pile of books to keep it flat.

If the frame is original the next thing to do is to clean the glass. There are many ways of doing this, but a good brand of modern window-cleaning liquid is usually the best thing to use. Clean well into the corners and do both sides. Put it away from any dust, and start on the frame. There will be the old backing-paper adhering to the back of this. Dampen it, and scrape off with a knife, until every tiny bit of it has gone. Wipe the back and inside edges of the frame, making quite sure that no small particles of paper remain, then polish the front of it. A silicon polish is good for gilt which should not be washed. Wooden frames should be polished with wax.

Now comes the exciting part. Return the glass to the frame, and polish, especially inside, with a silk duster, making quite sure that all finger-prints have been removed. Then put the sampler in, checking that it is the right way up in the frame! If it was originally framed with

Plate 9 Two straw-work caskets. The one on the left of the picture is of dyed straw-inlay on wood. The pincushion (*see below*) is covered with the original blue velvet; the one on the right has the undyed straw inlaid on cardboard and, relies entirely on the way the straw is laid to obtain the shaded effect. The drawer is lined with eighteenth-century wallpaper

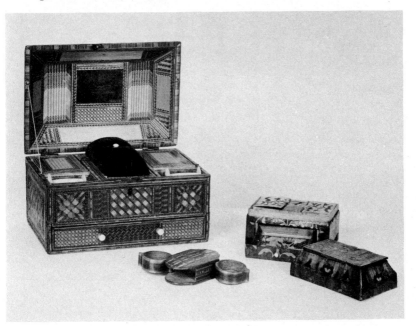

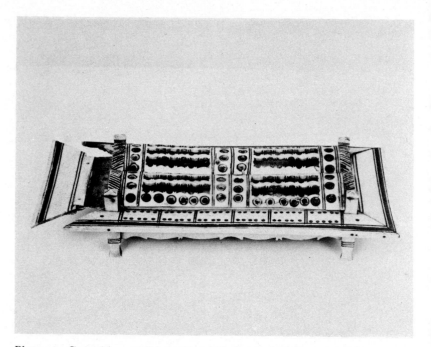

Plate 10 Carved bone cribbage-board, in form of a box containing dominoes and dice; (*below*) the picture on the interior lid is a French version of Wellington, with his troops in the background

a wooden backing, throw that away, and instead use a stout piece of white cardboard. Wood makes a very unsatisfactory backing. In the first place it gets very discoloured by age, and this discolouration is transferred to the sampler, and is the reason why so many antique samplers appear to have been worked on a khaki-coloured canvas. Secondly wood, especially if it is a thin wood, is a happy home for woodworms who work away unnoticed in the dark, finally boring holes in the sampler itself. Moths have a partiality for those worked in wool. Fasten the cardboard backing in with new brads, hammering them in gently, remembering old glass is fragile. Then cover over the edges where they meet the frame with white or brown gummed paper so as to render it dust-proof. Do not use Sellotape, as it peels off after a time.

If the sampler is of the later eighteenth-century period, a piece of paper may be found placed next to the back of the work, now very much discoloured with age. This should be removed, as it is doing the sampler no good, and a fresh piece of drawing-paper inserted. This will greatly improve the look of the sampler. When cleaning any antique framed needlework, be careful to examine any piece of wood or paper in the frame in case the history of the embroideress should be written on it; if on the stretcher, a careful copy should be made. If on the backing paper, this piece should be cut out and pasted on to the new piece. If on the frame itself, that particular part should be covered with a tough piece of cellophane instead of paper, to preserve it.

Mending Samplers

This is a hazardous job and, like marriage, not to be taken in hand lightly, inadvisedly or wantonly. If you are not a *very* good needle-woman, leave it alone, or get an expert to do it. As a matter of fact samplers suffer less than needlework pictures from decay. Apart from possible moth or worm holes, the hem-stitched edges of the canvas may become frayed. In the first event a piece of antique canvas of the same colour should be lightly stitched to the back of the canvas before framing. In the latter event a piece of antique linen tape about ¼in wide should be stitched all round the edge of the sampler so that it forms a firm border, before framing.

Faded Colours

Not very much can be done about this. Occasionally, however, certain colours will be found to have faded more than others, sometimes making the words almost illegible. If the sampler is held up to the light the words will become much clearer, and a copy should be made.

Silk-work Pictures

Eighteenth- and early nineteenth-century needlework pictures in silk are so well known as scarcely to need description. It would be difficult to 'discover' one in these enlightened days. Dirt would be the only real disguise.

Whereas in the early part of the eighteenth century the fashion had been to embroider on fine linen or canvas, towards the end of that century and on into the nineteenth, the rage was all for white or cream satin, or corded-silk backgrounds. Girls were now embroidering pictures instead of samplers and that is why it is easy for anyone familiar with this kind of work to find so much difference in the workmanship in the later period. All the immensely difficult raised French knots that were once used on tree work, could now be replaced by the use of 'chenille' thread, which could be made on a braid-loom, or bought ready-made from the haberdashers. It was a two-shaded green or brown furry-looking material with which foliage could easily be made, by using it in a sort of 'lazy daisy' stitch. Long 'tapestry' stitches were used for foregrounds and buildings.

'Dressed' Silk Pictures

Examine all eighteenth-century pictures worked in silks very carefully. If you are lucky you might come across a 'dressed' picture (Plate 5) in which the dresses of the ladies were actually pieces of material tacked in place on the silk background and the folds, gathers, tucks, etc, embroidered on the material. These 'dressed' pictures are extremely rare. In the mid-1930s a fashion sprang up of 'dressing' Victorian fashion prints by sticking appropriate materials on to the prints, and framing with the glass well away from the picture. These were quite effective and amusing, but although the prints may be prior to 1870, the actual work done on them was certainly not, therefore they cannot be considered genuine antiques.

Mending Silk Needlework Pictures

These present a far greater problem than samplers. The main difficulty arises when the embroidery has been done on a silk or satin background. All the main parts, ie the figures, trees, foreground, etc, will have been embroidered; but the faces of the figures, and the sky, will have been painted on to the background, and very often there are splits in it due to age. If the splits are slight, and the needlework of fine quality, it will not make much difference to the value of the picture, so on no account remove the picture from the frame, as exposure to air will only worsen the condition. Remove the dirty backing paper if necessary, and blow away any dust which may have gathered beneath it. Then put a clean piece of backing paper on. Always damp the paper before sticking it on, and it will then dry quite taut.

Hair Pictures

There are two or three different types of these, and they originated when superfine sewing silks and needles were invented. Fine black silks were used for making tiny stitches, almost in the manner of etching, and the subjects were almost always views of well-known country mansions – in many cases faithful copies of original etchings. In some cases real golden hair was used in place of silk to produce 'highlights'. This practice started the idea of making the whole of the picture in human hair of different colours. These were usually flower pictures worked on white satin and incorporating seed-pearls and gilt.

Hair was used extensively in the making of *mourning jewellery* – usually rings and small oval lockets – in which the deceased's hair was worked. But larger pieces were also made on parchment and framed in papier-mâché silhouette frames to hang as memorials (Plate 7). This work was often done by amateurs as well as professionals and how it was done is a mystery, for the only book on the subject I could find (a hand-written one) was 'missing' on both occasions I asked for it at a celebrated library. I suspect that some previous reader had wanted to take it home and have a longer look at it!

Mending

When the hair was not used in making tiny stitches it was 'couched' on in lengths. These couching stitches have worn away in many cases, and the hairs will be hanging loose. They should be couched on again, using a superfine needle and the finest possible silk.

Wool Work
Mending Wool-work Pictures

The damage to these has nearly all been done by moth, or wood-worm attacking through the back of the frame. The remedy is to remove the fragments of wool round the damaged parts with a very fine needle, and replace using the same stitch and a matching wool, on the same canvas. The difficulty is to find the right brand of wool in a colour which matches the original. I have found darning wool to be the answer to the colour problem. Owing to the introduction of manmade fibres hardly anything needs darning nowadays, so I beg the contents of long-forgotten 'darning bags' used by friends and relations when little samples of wool were provided with new woollen socks and jumpers. One can always use two strands of it if a thicker wool is required.

Strange to say the worst of all wools to match is a black one, owing to its fading properties. The Victorians were very apt to use black backgrounds to show up their brightly coloured flower work. It is now possible – and amusing – to see where they have run out of such background wool, and have obviously had to buy another make, which has not stood up to the light nearly so well as the original. My mother had an elegant walnut ottoman with an embroidered wool-work top (worked by her grandmother). The design was one of large brilliant coloured flowers, with a black background. When I was a girl I could never understand why parts of this background were worked in a sage-green as well as black!

Mending Other Wool Embroidery

In the seventeenth century wool was used for embroidering flowers, leaves, etc, on linen backgrounds for such things as bed-hangings and coverlets, and also for window curtains. In the eighteenth century it would seem to have been the practice of embroideresses to cut the wool embroidery away from the linen and transfer it to silk or velvet.

It was also fashionable in the eighteenth century to embroider the covers of upholstered chairs in wool embroidery. Usage, or moth, has since got to work on the plain coloured backgrounds of the embroidery but, rather than throw the whole cover away, a new modern method of preserving at least part of it, but based on the eighteenth-century appliqué, has been invented. The actual designs are cut or 'frayed' away from the background, a modern material of the original colour is used to re-cover the chair, and the designs are appliquéd on in the places they originally occupied. Photographs of the same chair taken before and after treatment show how very successful this method is.

Surely it would be a good idea to treat Victorian wool-work covers to chairs and stools in this way? If enough embroidery could not be salvaged to enable a whole chair to be re-covered, it would be admirable (appliquéd on to a suitable material) for the covers of 'drop-in' seats or even for cushion covers. It seems a pity to throw it away when it can be used again in this manner.

Felt Appliqué Work

There are two or three kinds of this work. Sometimes it takes the form of a flat bunch of multi-coloured flowers all made of applied felt or velvet, usually on a greyish-brown felt background. Sometimes it is a basket of fruit, the basket occasionally being in real basketwork and the fruit padded to give it the right shape. Each different fruit is made in the appropriate coloured felt or velvet, the 'shading' on each being done with embroidery. These confections are framed in a box frame, and are most attractive.

Another type is 'figure work', done with pieces of coloured material on a felt or paper background. Sometimes wool-work embroidery is used with this as the picture (Plate 5) of the boy and girl having a tiff. There was a famous exponent of figure work in the early nineteenth century – a tailor named Smart who lived at Frant near Tunbridge Wells. He made pictures with the bits of cloth, velvet, etc, left over from his trade, and his work became so widely known in that part of the world that it attracted the attention of the Duke of Sussex (one of the sons of George III). The latter became a patron of the delighted Mr Smart, who pasted labels on the back of his work, stating that he was under the patronage of the Duke of Sussex. 'Betty the Goose-woman' and 'Dick the Postman' were the most popular pair of pictures he did (Plate 6). His earliest were done on plain paper backings; after that, coloured prints of the district were used, showing Eridge Castle and Frant church. And a pair, now in America, had a water-colour painting of Smart's workshop at Frant as a backing. Any of these are eminently worth having.

A third type of felt work, and certainly the rarest, is embroidery combining human hair and silk. We once had a most beautiful example of this work. It was an oval portrait about 10in long, of the head of a young girl embroidered with very fine coloured silks on a dark-brown felt background. Her face in profile was beautifully worked, and her long fair hair was given an extra gloss because real human hair of the same colour had been incorporated, and had never lost its lustre. It was one of the most lovely, unforgettable things I have ever seen.

Mending Felt Work

Felt is very susceptible to moth, and if any crack has been left un-papered at the back of the frame it is an open invitation to them. If the moth-holes appear on the flowers or fruit a little judicious 'filling-in' stitch with embroidery silk will be the answer.

Moth-holes on the plain background are another matter. It was a great relief to me to find on one occasion that these occurred all round the edge of the picture near the frame. I solved the problem by covering them up with a piece of antique gold braid – which as a matter of fact improved the whole thing enormously!

Pieces of Old Damask or Brocade

Sometimes these are found in the guise of cushion covers made twenty or thirty years ago of antique materials, and now rather the worse for wear. Unpick the covers and see if any of the material is usable. If the colours are bright, and the material of the seventeenth or eighteenth century too delicate to repair, back it with net, and frame it in an old frame. It will really look delightful in the right place. If the pieces are repairable, darn where possible with a fine needle, using thread frayed out of the sides of the material.

Scraps of different coloured damask or brocade can be joined together with antique braid or velvet ribbon to make 'runners' for the tops of coffers, etc. Cut a piece of linen the right size and tack the strips on to it, with the raw edges close together. Then cover the joins with antique braid or ribbon. Turn in the material all the way round on to the linen, line – with old material if possible – and finish each end with fringe. It is a pity to throw away even quite small pieces of antique material. They can be used in so many ways: for lining old boxes for instance, or to stick underneath old coasters instead of the usual felt or baize.

If large pieces of antique material are found, it is always better to roll them round a roll of paper, before putting them away. Folding is inclined to make the piece wear out down each fold. It is advisable for anyone interested in antique materials to get accustomed, not only to antique designs and colours, but also to the way they hang. One must not touch them, but never neglect any opportunity of examining window and bed curtains in houses open to the public. Note the designs, colours, weave, etc. There are very informative books on fabrics which may be obtained from public libraries. But pictures of such things, even coloured pictures, cannot reveal the texture of the subject. Lovely bedspreads can be made from just enough antique material to cover the flat part of the bed. The sides can be formed by frills of a modern matching material.

It is worth remembering that all antique materials are useful things to collect. Bits of old canvas, lengths of linen tape, old interlinings and, what is even more important, old embroidery silks and sewing silks, for mending old materials or antique garments. Sometimes boxes of these scraps can be found in large house sales, or in the larger second-hand shops. It is sometimes worthwhile when visiting such places to buy up second-hand workboxes simply to obtain the contents.

Bead Work

This is a branch of needlework in which it would be quite possible to make an important and valuable discovery, because most people think of it as Victorian when it could just possibly be Stuart. Bead work was fashionable in the seventeenth century, when fine small china or glass beads of very bright colours were used, in embroidery, and in conjunction with fine wire, to make babies' layette-trays, and smaller baskets. The beauty of china beads is never lost, for the colours are fadeless. But they can accumulate centuries of dust and grime, which can easily be removed with soap and water. Stuart bead work is beautiful and intricate, but rarely seen outside museums and private collections. I did once, however, buy a small round bowl made of green and white beads on a wire base. It had been sold as Victorian, and because the beads were lack-lustre with the dirt of ages, no one recognised it for what it was.

In Regency days bead work became fashionable again, in embroidery. It was also done, very rarely, on wire; and we had a beautiful multi-coloured bead parrot, worked by threading the beads on a wire frame, of this period.

The craze for beads was revived in early Victorian times. Now the work was done quite differently. Instead of each bead being sewn on to the material separately, lines of them were strung on fine cotton thread, and stitched to the fabric between each bead. So no sewing on of separate beads was necessary except in certain cases. When it became necessary to do so, the beads were stitched on using a very fine needle. These superfine needles were supplied by the makers in small cardboard boxes hardly bigger than postage stamps. The edges were covered with gilt paper, and the tops covered by tiny Baxter prints in sepia or colours. The prints were made for the sake of convenience in long narrow strips (again like stamps) and were known as 'needle' prints – a confusing title, as some people have thought the actual print was produced in some way by needles. I have inherited a very fine papier-mâché box, once used by an ancestress for bead work. Lengths of tiny coloured beads threaded on fine cotton strings are in it, and several of these little needleboxes have been used to keep any odd beads in left over from finished work.

Beaded footstools were a necessity in most early Victorian drawing-rooms, as were the banners for pole screens. (These have been widely used to turn into cushion covers.) Other items made of bead work were bell-pulls and curtain-holders. Very occasionally one finds pictures worked entirely with beads. But it is more usual to find the beads combined with wool work.

Repairs to Bead-work Embroidery

What has usually happened where bead-work is exposed and often used, is that one of the threads holding a chain of beads has snapped and as the beads are not applied separately, this has loosened several more. The beads will be difficult to match in colour as well as size, and if the right kind of beads can be found, then no modern needle filled with modern silk will go through them. Use a piece of fine fuse-wire, thread your beads on to this, then fasten down by sewing the wire between each bead down to the background. If no matching beads can be found, cheat, by making French knots in embroidery silk to fill in the spaces. If the silk is carefully matched up with the beads, it will be difficult to tell the difference except at very close quarters.

Vestments and Altar Frontals

I have had many beautiful pieces of seventeenth- and eighteenth-century embroidered silk brocade to repair. In many cases the background has deteriorated so much that it has been necessary to transfer the embroidery to another fabric, matching it in colour and design as near as possible to the old one. New brocades are not much use – the colours are not the same, and the background design too modern. Skirts of Victorian ball gowns are what one needs here, or a simple modern material of corded silk. Some years ago I bought a late seventeenth- or early eighteenth-century chasuble, Spanish or Portuguese in origin, which had had this treatment (Plate 8). The magnificent embroidery which almost covered the entire vestment, had been transferred to a beautiful parma-violet coloured, finely ribbed silk and lined with the same coloured taffetas. The whole of the design was worked in silver and gold metal thread, with the exception of the faces of two cherubim at the bottom of the back of the chasuble. These were of solid silver. The appliqué work had been carried out with such cleverness that it was almost impossible to know it had been done at all. I imagine, by the fine quality of the corded silk and taffetas, that it had been done some time in the last century. And the embroideress signed her work, for two initials are worked in pale-blue silk at the bottom of the chasuble.

A great deal of very fine needlework and embroidery done on vestments and frontals has been discarded unnecessarily, simply because there was no one to do the work of transferring it. A good embroideress should really have no difficulty – the main thing is to anchor the embroidery here and there on the new material with a touch of adhesive, before sewing it on. It is very worthwhile and rewarding work which will last for years, and although it takes time, to my mind it is far, far better than the modern ready-made equivalents.

Tapestries

It is not often that one can discover such things. Everyone is aware of their value and if, and when, they should come up for sale, there is usually a ready market for them. But there is always an exception to prove a rule, and I would like to mention something that happened to us once.

We were, at one time, curators of the antique furniture at Bisham Abbey near Marlow. Our job was a very interesting one, and we much enjoyed our periodic visits there; unfortunately, owing to a quick succession of deaths, the very heavy death duties meant selling up the whole estate, and most of the antique contents of the abbey. The beautiful tapestries that had hung in the Great Hall were sold separately by a famous firm of auctioneers, but on our many visits I had noticed an interesting portière curtain, that was attached to a door in the part of the abbey occupied at one time by Miss Vansittart Neale, the former owner. I had a feeling that no one would notice this curtain, and that it would escape being 'lotted-up'. We could not bear to attend the sale, but later were called in to advise on what to do with the 'residue'. The curtain was one of the pieces in question and we were able to obtain it. It was, as I had guessed, an embroidered tapestry of the sixteenth century, not a woven one, and was beautifully worked in different coloured wools with long slanting stitches. At some time it had been cut right across and then seamed together again, but this did not destroy the picture, which portrayed a couple by a river in a vineyard, with a castle on a hill in the distance. The curtain was very dusty and in urgent need of professional repair and cleaning. After this had been done the transformation was astonishing, and I was delighted that we had been able to restore such a treasure.

Banners

During our time at the abbey I had to repair two ancient silk banners bearing armorial crests, that had belonged to the Vansittart family and had always hung from the gallery in the Great Hall. These were very battered and frayed and it was quite impossible to darn them in any way as the material was much too fragile. After much thought I covered them on both sides with a fine brown nylon net and carefully stitched the net together between the fragments so that they were enclosed in the net, and could not drop away. When the banners were rehung one did not see the net at all, it merged unnoticed into the atmosphere. And the historic silk banners were saved for a few years longer. A tedious job, but worthwhile.

Lace

Lace is almost sure to be found stored away somewhere in old houses in the form of collars, cuffs, half-sleeves, fichus, scarves, mittens, jabots, cravats and caps. Even larger pieces such as Honiton shawls and veils, and whole skirts. For some reason or other lace is not considered valuable. Dealers declare it to be a 'drug on the market', though why, I have never been able to find out. It is antique, hand-made, very beautiful, and yet thoroughly neglected. I do not think, however, that it will remain so for long. Someone is sure to 'discover' it, and then up will go the price. There are so many things that can be done with lace that I wonder the public at large, or informed bodies such as the Women's Institutes, have not discovered them. I bought a cardboard carton full of old embroidered muslin and lace scraps for £1 from an Oxfam shop. Some of it was immediately usable in the form of collars, and I dressed an antique baby doll with the embroidered muslin. Other pieces I gave to a church embroideress to mend the lace on vestments and alter frontals and cloths. She was highly delighted. Real lace cannot be mended, or even replaced, with the kind of nylon substitute that is all one can buy today. Narrow Valenciennes lace that has been stitched on to frills can be unpicked, washed and ironed carefully, and sewn on to lawn or linen ready-made handkerchiefs for presents. A best dress for a baby or little girl can be trimmed with it. Buckinghamshire lace can transform the ends of a plain linen traycloth. And a really fine piece of lace backed by a good coloured plain material and framed in an antique frame would give pleasure to many female antique collectors. There are numberless ways in which these scraps of old lace can be used; if I had the time I would make a patchwork quilt of coarse hand-made lace mounted on coloured linen. I do not advise cushion covers done in this way because they would get too much wear to be practical, but small lampshades for porcelain lamps would be delightful.

Washing and Repairing Old Lace

Old lace can be very fragile and must be treated with considerable care. A great deal of what is left to us is in detached garments such as caps, collars and cuffs, fichus, scarves, jabots and sleeve frills. The best way of washing these is to put them in a wide-topped jar partly filled with warm soapy water, not detergent, and shake them about. Rinse in the same way and dry flat on a Turkish towel, gently pulling and smoothing them into shape. Hand-made lace was never ironed. A great deal was made before flat-irons were invented, and afterwards irons were not used for fear of the point entangling the lace, or the danger of scorching through using too hot an iron. Lace rollers were used for flattening flat pieces of lace. These were shaped like ordinary pastry rollers but with tapering ends, and were made of a smooth polished wood. The lace was half dried in a dry towel, and then wrapped, right side downwards, round and round the roller. When dry, the roller was rolled over and over on a clean cloth, and the lace then slipped off the end of the roller and was put away in the lace box or stitched back into place on the garment.

If the lace is attached to the garment, iron it very carefully on the wrong side, pulling it into shape as you do so. The iron should not be too hot. The lace trimming should be ironed first in this way, and the garment afterwards with a hotter iron.

Mending old lace is really a needlework-expert's job. Her main difficulty nowadays will be to find old thread to use of the same fineness as the original. On no account should nylon thread be used. I have been asked how one tells the difference between antique and modern lace. This is easy if, by modern, nylon lace is meant. Nylon lace is coarse and stiff looking. Old lace for personal garments is very fine and delicate – although Buckinghamshire hand-made lace for edging towels, etc, would naturally be of coarser cotton. It is more difficult to tell the difference between hand-made lace and machine-made lace made before nylon thread was invented. But even machine-made lace of this period is so very superior to nylon lace that it is worth preserving.

Anyone really interested in antique lace should learn as much as possible about the subject. Most public libraries have a book or two about it. It is a fascinating study.

5 Antiques in Old Houses

In Attics and Cellars

These parts of an old house have always held a great fascination for me ever since, at a very impressionable age, I lived in an old Georgian house just outside a big town in the Midlands. It was the kind of house I had always liked to draw – three storeys high, with an important front door in the middle with a window on either side of it. There were two steps leading up from the pavement to the front door, which had a tethering ring, once used for horses, at the side of the brass bell-pull. There were three windows across each of the upper two storeys, and the whole was finished by a steeply sloping slate roof with an imposing number of chimney pots. Inside, as well as the usual sort of accommodation, were two staircases, a passage leading to a side door and lobby, semi-basement kitchens, attics and cellars.

About three times a year, as a great treat, my father would take us round the attics. It was rather a precarious procedure, for in some places it was quite easy to put one's foot through the ceiling of the room below. Also there was no light laid on up there, and so he lit the way romantically with a candle. I suppose, on looking back, that though one could walk about up there all over the house, most of the space must have been service lofts for emergencies such as broken slates or frozen tanks, and that there were only two real attics. Access was through a little door at the top of a short flight of stairs on the nursery landing, but we were forbidden to go up there by ourselves. Why these attics had such a fascination for us I do not know. There was nothing at all interesting in them. All that had ever been found there was a Victorian toilet set in flowered china. But although they contained no treasure, no skeletons in chests, nor even an interesting-looking trunk, they certainly seemed romantic to us.

The cellars were much more rewarding. They were very deep down, under the basement kitchens. One was a wine cellar – quite empty – and from that the way went through a door and down a circular staircase cut out of the rock. This led to a kind of cellar-cave which had a seat, also cut out of the rock, three-quarters of the way round it. Near the entrance, held by an iron stanchion embedded deep in the rock, was a sinister-looking iron chain. It seemed to us that it had quite certainly been put there to secure some wretched prisoner; and I should not now be surprised to learn that that was exactly what it was for. The circular staircase and the rock-cellar were so much older than the rest of the house that it is more than probable that it had been built on medieval foundations. Unfortunately no one now will ever know the answer, for that part of the town was very heavily bombed during World War II, and everything razed to the ground. Another old house we stayed in for a short time in the same town was a seventeenth-century mansion. The attics here were used as bedrooms, but there was a much earlier rock-cellar which had a well in it. Over this, carved in rock, was a grotesque and rather frightening head.

Writing of wells reminds me that a great many wells in old houses and gardens are still there, and remain undiscovered until unexplained damp stone floors, or extensive digging in gardens, brings them to light. An early well was discovered in the middle of the lawn belonging to an ancient house in Eton. Unhappily, it had to be filled in, but I was taken to see it before this happened. It was extremely interesting, with chalk foundations and Tudor brick work at the top. Another early well was discovered in the gardens of an old house at Windsor during gardening operations. I was told this when the lady who had discovered it brought me an object she had fished up from the bottom. This was and eighteenth-century brown earthenware chamber-pot not damaged in any way! What it was doing at the bottom of a well neither of us could imagine, but I found out later – in quite another connection and with an early photograph to prove it – that Buckinghamshire lace makers used these receptacles as foot-warmers, by putting red-hot embers into them and placing them between their feet, with their long skirts pulled down over them. Perhaps the embers flared up unexpectedly, and the 'foot-warmer' had to be rushed into the garden and thrown down the well to extinguish the flames.

The house we lived in at Marlow was an Elizabethan one with a Queen Anne front. In the loft there we found some very original antiques. There was an eighteenth-century adjustable padded bed-rest, and some very interesting tailor's account books of the early nineteenth century, which not only made fascinating reading, but gave an Austen-like glimpse of life in and around the town at that period. The tailor who had once occupied the house, seemed to earn most of his income by making liveries for the servants at all the large houses in the neighbourhood – and very colourful some of them were. Here and there we came across entries 'for making an overcoat for young master . . .'. (The country tailor could evidently be trusted to make the clothes of those members of the family still in the schoolroom.) Being a parson's daughter I was much interested in the occasional entries 'for mending the vicar's cassock 2s 6d', perhaps all the poor vicar could afford, for he never seemed to have a new one.

The cellars of this old house were not particularly interesting but very handy because we used them as bargain basements where we could sell all the odd lots we had to buy at sales in order to obtain one worthwhile article. There was a great demand in the 1930s for very small chests-of-drawers. In order to satisfy our customers, we used to buy the kind of mahogany bedside commode which was disguised as a chest-of-drawers, by having dummy drawer-fronts complete with handles. These our cabinet maker made into real drawers with old wood, but normally we had to get rid of the 'commode' parts first, so down into the bargain basement went the tall white china pots (the shape of Welsh ladies' top-hats) and down our area steps toddled the old ladies from the alms houses, who were in urgent need of replacements, having been told by our daily that they were being given away. They certainly discovered useful antiques in a cellar!

In our fifteenth-century premises at Eton we have a large loft reached by a ladder. It has always been my ambition to build a proper staircase up to it, for it would make a wonderful room, but it would be a large and dusty undertaking, and difficult to do in a house always open to the public. There is, to quote a well-used phrase, 'a wealth of old beams' up there. When we first ventured through the trap-door after we had bought the house, we found there was also a wealth of large bats, all clinging to the old beams. It was a most alarming sight and I am thankful to say that they soon disappeared.

There was also at that time a loft over the room in the front of the house, but the ceiling beams which seemed inadequately attached to the side beams, started to come away, and as an ominous crack appeared in the ceiling we had to have the whole loft removed, both for the sake of the customers and our antique furniture. The builder, who knew all about the vagaries of Eton architecture, was of the opinion that the loft had not been part of the original building, but put in afterwards, probably when the back part of the house had been added in the sixteenth century. This was quite obvious when the ceiling had been taken down, and it was discovered that the two end gables were plastered; which would not have been the case had the loft always been there. There was no proper entrance to it either, though one might have squeezed through by the side of the chimney. It crossed my mind that we might have discovered a 'hide', for it is well known that such places were made during the religious persecutions in England in the sixteenth century, legitimate building operations carried out at the same time providing the necessary cover for the construction. Incidentally, since the ceiling plaster was old, having been made partly of cow dung, the amount of dust that ensued during its being pulled down was appalling. Even though the door was kept shut and heavy dust sheets hung over the outside of it, the dust seeped through and permeated the whole building. When it was being swept up preparatory to being carted away, the workmen flung both parts of the casement window wide open, with the result that clouds and clouds of thick dust were blown out across the street. There were two American ladies in the shop at the time, and I was explaining what was going on overhead when a man suddenly rushed across the street and, thrusting the door open, said excitedly, 'The house is on fire! There are clouds of smoke pouring out of your upstairs window.' I thanked him very much, and explained that it was merely sixteenth-century dust, and for all I knew there might be plague germs in it. I am sure he thought I was pulling his leg, but the American ladies were highly amused at the whole incident!

The cellar under the back part of the house was itself a real discovery. We had no idea that one existed, until the floor began to sink near the window, where there was a heavy oak writing-desk. The builders pulled up a board or two, and announced that the dampness of the cellar below was the cause of the trouble! I should explain that this house is the end one of a group of five, built sometime around 1420 by a man named Strugnell. The ground-floor then consisted of open shops, the first being an alehouse, followed by a bakery, a butcher's, a grocer's and a leather seller's. According to one authority the room over the alehouse was used as a council chamber and that was why it was higher and more important than the others. All the upstairs rooms ran into each other, the staircase leading to them being in the bakehouse. The whole row was only one room thick, but in the sixteenth century other rooms were added at the back, and a cellar for brewing was made underneath the alehouse, which continued to be used as such until the beginning of the seventeenth century. It was known as the 'Adam and Eve'.

The cellar was a good sound brick-built one, 8ft deep, 19ft long, and 9ft wide. The floor to the room above was renewed in Victorian times, and no access from there was made to the cellar, which was reached by a 'brewer's hatch' out in the yard. When the house was 'modernised' in 1951 by removing lathe and plaster from this room, and replacing all the Victorian sash windows with leaded casement ones, all the resultant debris was thrown down into the cellar. The flap was then concreted over and the cellar was thus hermetically sealed. What the modernisers had not realised was that, when the river rises above a certain level, the cellars are apt to get flooded, and this is what

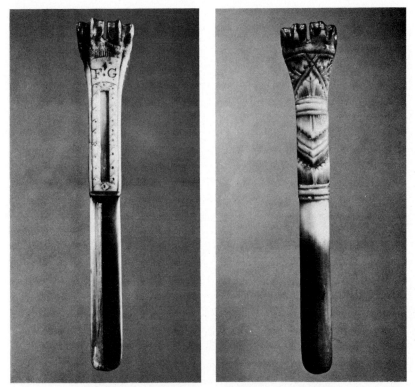

Plate 11 (*above*) Apple-corer of carved and shaded knuckle bone, bearing the owner's initials. The blade is stained with apple juice; (*below left*) early eighteenth-century English doll's or 'baby' house made to show off the precious miniature toys of an adult. It is now used to house part of the author's collection of eighteenth- and early nineteenth-century miniature brass furniture; (*below right*) back of the house, showing the door with original iron butterfly hinges

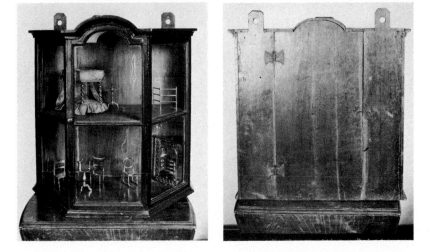

Plate 12 (*above left*) An early love token in the shape of a heart. The 'wheel' is incorporated in the carving. It measures about 4in in length; (*above right*) the reverse side of the same love token bears one of the earliest dates known for such things – 1641; (*below*) a sailor's shell 'Valentine'. These were not actually made by sailors, but bought ready-made in Barbados to take home as 'Valentines' after visiting the West Indies

had happened. The water had come into the cellar and made a horrible porridge of the rubbish there, and that was what caused the floor above to sink. It all had to be cleared and out of the mass of rubbish only two things were salvaged – a Georgian military sword with the point broken off, and an early oak standing-candlestick. We sold the latter but kept the former as a memento, and now use it for poking the fire. There is now a trap-door and wooden staircase leading to the cellar, which is very entertaining for our young visitors. There must have been cellars at Bisham Abbey, near Marlow, but in the days when we operated there we never had reason to visit them. We did, however, penetrate into the tower garret – an uncomfortably stuffy place – and found many valuable antiques which had been stored up there, possibly during the refurnishing of the refectory in early Victorian days. There was a set of Chippendale period mahogany dining chairs, several oil paintings and old prints, large carved gilt frames, odd Hepplewhite armchairs, and various pieces of furniture which needed repair, all under a heavy coating of dust, and with the stuffing coming out of the chairs. This was quite a valuable haul and, strangely enough, no one had thought the things were of much value, and they were not even listed in the original inventory. I suppose to the uninitiated it would look like a lot of mouldy old rubbish, and might even have been sold as such, if it had not been discovered and brought to life again.

It is not everyone, however, who has a sixteenth-century attic in which to make such discoveries. What one hopes to find in more prosaic attics and boxrooms are nineteenth-century travelling trunks with domed tops filled with garments from another age. Things that were once too old-fashioned to wear, yet too good to throw away. At the present time such garments are fetching good prices in high-class sale rooms – not only bought by collectors, museums and theatrical outfitters, but by discerning people who buy them for the sake of the materials which are matchless in these days of man-made fibres. I have been lucky enough to know at least two attics where such things were kept. One, as well as at least two trunks, had two pieces of antique furniture: a Jacobean chest-of-drawers, and a Sheraton mahogany bureau. One of the trunks was filled with clothes of the early nineteenth century. Ball gowns, day dresses, a hand-embroidered white muslin wedding dress, a collapsible crinoline frame and bustle. There were hats, bonnets and parasols. The excitement of trying everything on was immense. Another attic had a trunk full of 'dressing-up clothes', both male and female, which had been used for charades and plays. Such

E

houses have changed I know, some have been turned into flats – even the attics – but there must still be a great many places where clothes handed down in the family have been stored away and forgotten. We still have the clothes that great-grandfather Toller wore at his wedding in 1846. They seem to have been worn very little. Perhaps married life agreed with him so well that he began to put on weight, and grew out of them!

Other things one finds stored away in boxes are old letters, diaries, bills, copybooks, early cooking recipes written in lovely Italic script on hand-made paper and old Victorian songs with pictures on the back (which makes it worthwhile going through piles of dusty music to find something now valuable, that was carted up to the attic when singing for one's own pleasure went out of fashion). I hear from time to time of more unusual and valuable things than these being discovered in most extraordinary places. For instance, at a recent house sale there were in the outbuildings, boxes of sundries such as old tennis shoes and nets. A friend, who believes in going through everything, in the hope that something of interest may turn up in the end, turned one out to find that right at the bottom were two Roman mural gravestones, dated and named. He carefully put back the canvas shoes and old tennis nets on top of them again, and secured the lot for the proverbial song.

In Roof Timbers, Fireplaces, Cupboards and Behind Panelling

Apart from cellars and attics other parts of a house can be the site of strange discoveries. At Chawton in Hampshire there is an old house which was once occupied by a fellow antique dealer. He showed us some old shoes which he had found in his roof timbers. They had been put there purposely, as doing so was supposed to bring luck to the occupiers.

There is always the chance of finding something when a bricked-up fireplace is opened out, even if it is only a bread oven placed high up at one side of an open hearth. A large bricked-up fireplace was opened up some years ago in the front room of a house in Spittal Street, Marlow. Not only was the very big open hearth discovered, but a fascinating little latticed window built in the left-hand side of the back of it. This had originally been intended to give light to anyone sitting in the inglenook. The curious thing was that nobody seemed to have noticed it on the outside. Under this room was a stone crypt, with a vaulted ceiling, much earlier than the house itself. This probably had been part of the Hospice (or hospital) of the Knights of St John, which had occupied part of Spittal Street in the Middle Ages. The curious name of this street was, of course, a corruption of the word 'hospital'. A friend living in a delightful old house in Broadway, Worcestershire, decided to pull out the modern grate in one of his living-rooms and found two more behind it. The first had a hob grate with a carved pine surround in the Adam manner, and behind that was the original Tudor open hearth.

Old ancient cupboards are usually worth looking into, though dusty and the haunt of spiders. We bought a valuable set of eight Elizabethan banquet roundels in the original box, in most beautiful condition; but on top of the roundels was a note in Victorian writing to say they had been found in the back of a deep cupboard in a large old house in Yorkshire that had for many years been used as a nunnery. The box had remained there unnoticed all through the nuns' occupation, though I do not suppose the dear good ladies would have realised what the roundels were, even if they had found them. They are now in the Bristol Museum.

Many cupboards in Victorian days, especially those near a fireplace, were papered over to give the room a more symmetrical look, in accordance with the taste of the time. Every time the room was re-papered the cupboards got an extra covering, and ultimately were quite forgotten. I have found these cupboards occasionally, but must confess they were quite empty.

Interesting discoveries can be made behind layers of wallpaper, behind panelling or disguised under layers of paint, on the panelling itself. About twenty-five years ago some very ancient houses in Eton High Street were pulled down to make an entrance into the car park. An old-established antique dealer lived in one of them and his son told me that when one of the front upstairs rooms was being demolished, it was discovered that the walls had originally been covered with embossed painted leather – over this were several layers of wallpaper. The old gentleman salvaged as much as possible before the whole edifice was brought tumbling down. I believe he had the fragments framed, turning them into pictures; and his son told me that the leather, when cleaned, was bright and glowing. The whole room must have been a wonderful sight in its heyday. There are very few of these leather-covered walls, and these particular ones could have been restored, or at any rate more of the leather saved, had its owner been aware of their existence.

A happier case of decorated walls being restored to their former brilliance occurred in an early sixteenth-century house in Sussex. Here there was an upstairs room panelled in pine, which had been grained to imitate oak. It was decided to remove this, starting with the panel over the chimney-piece. This led to the discovery of a sixteenth-century painted seascape. Immediately an expert was called in, and the graining was very carefully removed from each panel. It was then discovered that the whole of the upper half of the room was painted, each with a different rural scene. Previously it had been rather a dull little room; when it was finished it became a room of colourful delights, and I had the satisfaction of seeing it before, during and after its transformation. I was also present just after some much earlier murals were discovered on the plaster wall behind the panelling in an early fifteenth-century house in the Cotswolds.

In the time of Queen Anne it was fashionable to paint the oak panelling in old houses with light colours, to make the rooms lighter and more in keeping with the walnut furniture of the period. Successive owners will have repainted the panelling ever since, so that it is a good idea, when a house is known to have been built before the eighteenth century, to test the paint on the panelling, before becoming too energetic with the stripper. Something much more beautiful and exciting might inadvertently be stripped off with the paint! But, if any discovery of this sort is made, it is as well to call for the services of an expert. Restoration of this kind should never be attempted by amateurs.

Sometimes one finds hidden cavities behind panelling, but I have never met anyone who found a treasure in such a place. Yet they are not always empty, as the following story, told me by a distant relation when I was a girl, will prove. She had the story from her grandmother, who was an eye-witness of the event as a child. Having lost both her parents when very young, this grandmother had been brought up by her paternal grandparents, who lived in an ancient family mansion in a remote part of Cumberland. She remembered very well that at times when she sat by the fireplace in the Great Hall, she would hear a tap-tap, tap-tap, on the panelling by her side. She asked several members of the household what it was, and was told variously that it was 'mice in the wainscoting', 'crickets on the hearth', 'bits of plaster falling down behind the panelling'. But none of these suggestions seemed to answer her question satisfactorily. To her it seemed like someone knocking to be let out, and if she were in the room by herself when it happened, she would run off somewhere else as the noise frightened her. Then there came a time when various parts of the fabric of the old house needed repair, and workmen were called in. Something on the side of the Great Hall chimney needed attention, and part of the panelling near the hearth had to be removed. The child was in the room at the time watching the proceedings. The workmen stopped work suddenly and began to mutter together, then one of them was sent to fetch the master, who was told that they had found a cavity behind the panelling, and there seemed to be something in it. Her grandfather came, looked inside, and then put his hand into the cavity and drew something out. She never forgot what she saw. It was a mummified hand cut off at the wrist, the fingers curling inwards. It had been hanging from a cord, so that any sudden draught from the chimney, blowing through into the cavity, would set it tap-tapping against the panelling. She had been right. It was not 'mice behind the wainscoting', nor 'crickets on the hearth', nor yet 'bits of plaster'. The relic was given a Christian burial in the churchyard and, although every effort was made to find out, it had all happened too long ago for anyone to remember anything about it. The secret of the dark and terrible deed was never discovered.

6 Papier-mâché, Pontypool Ware, and Prisoner-of-War Work

Papier-mâché

Papier-mâché is very popular nowadays, not only with collectors, but because it comes under the heading of Victoriana, therefore many papier-mâché articles can be discovered in 'Victoriana' shops (Plate 8). Although in England articles have been made from this composition since at least the seventeenth century, most people imagine it to be solely a Victorian product, and for this reason a short history of it may not come amiss.

Up to about the middle of the eighteenth century, it was almost certainly produced mainly by amateurs, but in 1765 the Rev C. T. Crowther, in his book *The Complete Dictionary of the Arts*, gave directions for making the paper-pulp process. His method was to mix paper-pulp with glue, chalk and fine sand, and then to press it by hand into oiled boxwood moulds. After being baked until hard, the article was then ready for japanning. At this time the manufacture was called 'paper-ware'. It was not until the next century that Jennens & Bettridge gave it the name of 'papier-mâché'. A celebrated printer, John Baskerville of Birmingham (1702–75), as well as two other men, Stephen Bedford and John Taylor, were all experimenting in making paper-ware articles – not with pulp, but with several sheets of paper pasted together. Stephen Bedford also was experimenting with varnishes, and finally produced an excellent one which was hard, transparent and not liable to crack. This was called 'copal varnish', and was used thereafter by most firms for the purposes of japanning.

Baskerville had made great strides with his paper-ware experiments and, when he retired, his apprentice Henry Clay continued with the experiments until at last, in 1772, he was able to produce a new heat-resisting paper-ware so hard that it could be treated in exactly the same way as wood – sawn, dovetailed, screwed, etc. This was a most important discovery, for ever since lacquer cabinets had been imported into England, via Holland, from the East in the late seventeenth century, experiments had been going on to produce a substance like wood that would not warp or crack with the excessive heat of the baking ovens used in this country to harden the lacquer. In Eastern countries lacquered articles were dried out-of-doors in caves, but this method was impractical in the English climate. Ovens had to be used for baking, and often the wood employed in making the cabinets would be cracked or warped during the process. Henry Clay's improved paper-ware was a great success, and after his patent expired every good manufacturer of this product used his formula for making it. And thus

83

was established one of the most important trades in the Midlands of that time.

When Henry Clay transferred his business to Covent Garden, London, in 1792, his Birmingham factory was taken over by Small & Son, Guest, Chopping & Bill, who worked it until 1816 when it was taken over by Jennens & Bettridge. This firm achieved fame, not only by the exellence of their workmanship, but by their invention of inlaying with mother-of-pearl. Pearl inlay had been invented by Henry Clay but, whereas his method was really to inlay the pearl in papier-mâché, theirs was to stick the pearl on with adhesives, and then give the article as many coats of varnish as would bring it up level with the pearl. Any residue of the varnish was then wiped off the pearl and the piece given a final polish. Jennens & Bettridge were particular to use a strong adhesive, and very thin mother-of-pearl; both have stood the test of time, for very few missing pieces are ever found on articles of their manufacture, whereas on the cheaper varieties whole chunks of it have often come away.

The firm had an enormous output of goods, from small trays to large pieces of furniture. They employed well-known artists to paint the goods for them and who were not allowed to sign their work. They used an impressed mark on their articles – the name 'Jennens & Bettridge' with a crown, signifying that they were under royal patronage; thus following the example of Henry Clay who impressed his name, and later the words 'Covent Garden' and a crown. It is a known fact that both firms signed all their work. Much unsigned work, especially with regard to trays, has often been attributed to these two early makers, but it is never safe to make such an attribution to an unsigned article.

Papier-mâché was also made at Wolverhampton, the most noted maker being Benjamin Walton. He joined the firm of William Ryton in 1810, and became the sole proprietor in 1842. In 1850 he was succeeded by his son Fred Walton, who carried on the business for another thirty years. During this time the fame of the firm was due partly to the excellence of the decoration, which consisted of beautifully painted flowers and exotic birds on a background of pale bronze. The gilding used with this decoration was of the finest quality, and such decorated trays are often hung on walls in lieu of pictures. The mark 'B Walton Warranted' was impressed on the back of this firm's work in bold lettering. The Wolverhampton factories were famous for this bronze decoration which adorned not only trays but tall urn-shaped vases. They did not use mother-of-pearl for the decoration of papier-mâché.

There were other firms operating in Birmingham and Wolverhampton who marked their work. Also firms with factories in other towns. Spiers & Son, Oxford, was a celebrated example of how to achieve fame the easy way. This firm did not actually manufacture papier-mâché, but had the brilliant idea of buying small pieces of furniture, trays, etc, in the 'blank' (ie undecorated) from Birmingham manufacturers and, working from studios, hired accomplished gilders and proficient artists to decorate the articles. These were signed 'Spiers & Son, Oxford', the words being painted at the edge of the picture, usually a view of one of the Oxford colleges. There was one notable exception – that of Windsor Castle. This particular subject can be found painted on the round trays with ormulu handles, usually described as card or cake trays, though they were actually intended to hold the balls of Berlin wool used in the fashionable embroidery of the period. The firm of Spiers displayed all this really fine work under their own name as manufacturers, at all the important exhibitions.

Hints on Buying and Cleaning Papier-mâché

It will not be easy to find a bargain, but search for the early kind of papier-mâché made before 1870: such things as trays, snuffers-trays, wine-coasters, small workboxes and inkstands. The later shoddy variety was specially made to sell cheaply, consequently it is light in weight and badly lacquered, and any pearl decoration is usually carried out in 'chips' or unattractive blobs. Such stuff is not worth discovering.

Dirt will be the main disguise. Use a thin white liquid cream which will clean as well as polish or, in extremely dirty cases, an all-purpose household cleanser. Be sparing of water. If it is absolutely necessary to use it, dry with a soft cloth and polish immediately. The expensive white polish mentioned on page 34 is also very good to use on papier-mâché as it is almost finger-print proof. When the article has been cleaned and polished, remember never to display it in a strong light – sunlight is fatal, especially to papier-mâché with a black background, which in a short time will be turned to a dirty looking grey, and all the original polish will be taken from the lacquer. All too often I have seen beautiful pieces of pristine papier-mâché completely ruined by being placed in the strong sunlight of shop windows.

Do not be too fussy about a piece being marked. This craze for wishing to label everything 'Henry Clay' or 'Jennens & Bettridge' has resulted in faked marks now being impressed on articles, obviously without any knowledge of the kind of manufacture the firm did, or the period in which it was made. I give three instances:

1 a really beautiful and quite perfect oval tea-tray which according to shape and decoration was *circa* 1850, being marked 'Henry Clay'

2 a snuffers-tray of black with delicate gilding, *circa* 1770, being marked 'Jennens & Bettridge'

3 a very late counters-box (originally one of a set of five), made in Japan but marked with the early mark of Jennens & Bettridge

These faked marks were presumably made with a hot iron, and the surrounding papier-mâché then sand-papered to take away any rough edges. The joke is that the Henry Clay has been given a Victorian shaped crown, and the Jennens & Bettridge a Georgian one.

Beware of late paintings on early trays. A great many early trays (including those of Henry Clay) had only the border painted. The main portion of the tray, where the tea-service would stand, was left undecorated. Unfortunately, in the 1930s the American fashion was for all-over decoration on papier-mâché trays. As these were rare, demand had to be met somehow, and there were studios in Chelsea which set out to help the export drive by painting coaching, hunting and flower pictures in oils on the blank interiors of really lovely trays. No trouble was taken to see that the style or type of brushwork even vaguely resembled the exquisite paintings on the edges or border-work. Consequently terrible blunders were made; and I have had the unpleasant task of having to tell more than one proud possessor of a tray made, decorated and marked by Henry Clay, that the whole of the painting of the inner panel was a fake, and the tray consequently of no great value. Beware also of faked paintings on chair-backs, trays and blotters, that turn out merely to be coloured prints attached to the article and then well varnished. This was done on the late papier-mâché articles to save cost of painting.

Jewel-cases, crochet boxes, etc, are often found with damaged hinges, or the hinges broken away from the boxes. These can sometimes be mended by a clever amateur; but if the piece is a good one, it is better to get an 'antique' cabinet-maker to mend it. Sometimes the hinges have only one side that screws on to the box, the rest of the hinge being a 'flap' that fits into a socket. The socket is apt to become enlarged, and this 'flap' then comes away from it. This hole can be filled with plastic wood, and the flap pressed back into it. Wipe away all excess filling, shut the box, put a couple of books on it to keep the lid down tight, and leave for twenty-four hours to set. Never use Sellotape on the surface of papier-mâché; it leaves an ineradicable mark – so do sticky price labels!

Any good piece where the painting is ruined by old and dirty varnish can be treated in exactly the same way as a picture suffering from the same complaint. The lacquer or varnish should be removed by an expert picture restorer, and then the piece should be re-varnished. Do not grudge the money spent on this operation, for if the piece is a good one to begin with, it should be worth the cost. A few years ago a friend of mine bought a beautifully painted large round papier-mâché tray at an antique dealers fair, for which she paid £9. Unfortunately, the varnish was very dirty and badly scratched, and almost hid the painting of exotic birds and flowers with which the tray was decorated. On my advice she had this tray treated by an expert. He charged a very reasonable price, and the result astonished and delighted her. It would now cost very considerably more to buy than she paid both for the tray and its restoration, so she certainly had discovered a bargain.

Sometimes pieces of mother-of-pearl are missing from what would otherwise be a good piece. I believe it is possible to get thin sheets of mother-of-pearl from which to fill in the empty spaces. A template of the piece needed should be made in some thin waterproof fabric because, in order to avoid a lot of 'splitting' when the mother-of-pearl is cut, the operation should be done under water with a sharp pair of scissors.

Pontypool or Enamelled Tinware

This really beautiful material was first invented at Pontypool in Monmouthshire, where a family called Allgood had had an ironfoundry since the seventeenth century. In the search for a material that could be used instead of wood for lacquering, thin iron plates had been suggested. But iron was found to be a bad surface for enamelling on. In 1730 Edward Allgood had the idea of tinning these thin iron plates, and it turned out to be a remarkable success, for all kinds of objects could be made of this tinware, which could be easily cut, moulded and lacquered. Trays, chestnut-urns, candlesticks, wine-coasters, and snuffers-trays were produced in large quantities, not only for home consumption, but for export abroad to Europe, America and even Russia. The earliest known dated piece of Pontypool tinware is a clock dial made in 1742. Two of Edward Allgood's sons opened a rival factory at Usk, a few miles away, and business was carried on there until the 1870s, when the last remaining Allgood emigrated to America.

This tinware was also made at Wolverhampton, Bilston and Birmingham, and a thriving trade was done in it both at home and abroad. It was still referred to, however, as 'Pontypool'. Strange to say, despite all this, one nowadays more often than not hears it referred to as 'tôle', the French counterpart. A firm called Shoolbridge, Loveridge & Co was making it at Wolverhampton in 1850. From 1862 to 1904 it was made by H. Loveridge & Co who supplied goods to William Whiteley, when his famous emporium was first opened. We once found a most amusing toilet set, comprising jug and basin, soap and toothbrush dishes, chamber-pot, slop-pail and foot-bath. All were decorated with a bold design of red poppies on a black lacquer background, but each utensil was enamelled white inside. The interesting feature of this set was that, not only did it bear the trade mark and registration number of the Loveridge firm, but Whiteley's trade mark as well. The date, revealed by the diamond-shaped registration number, was somewhere in the 1870s. It had probably been made to place on the wash-stand of one of the papier-mâché bedroom suites that were being made at Birmingham at this time.

Fine tinware made at Wolverhampton was so well lacquered that, at first glance, it could be taken for the best papier-mâché of the same period. The earnest would-be 'discoverer' need not give up hope of finding any, though it may take a good deal of looking for. In the last six months I have found two outstanding pieces: one a blue lacquered tin snuffers-tray, decorated with small beautifully painted pink roses; and the other – the rarest piece I have ever seen – an oval black lacquer tray, about 15in long with an outstandingly fine gilded border about 2in deep. It is in pristine condition, the back of the tray being covered with a piece of thick white felt to protect it from wear, and on this is pasted a list of sizes and prices in which the tray could be obtained – unfortunately the maker's name was not given. This is obviously a salesman's sample, and is as fresh and new looking as when it came from the factory.

It seems rather curious that Wolverhampton manufacturers would never use mother-of-pearl as a decoration on papier-mâché, but they did not object to using it on tinware which one would think was not nearly such an appropriate material for such treatment.

Dirt will be the main disguise of Pontypool tinware. But in the later and cheaper kind made at Wolverhampton, where to save cost the coats of lacquer were reduced to a minimum, rust will be the trouble. Constant usage wore the lacquer down on the edges of trays for instance, and the tin becomes exposed to damp, etc, and rust sets in. This can be doctored by gently rubbing with the very finest glass-paper, and then matching up the colour, using artists' oil paints, applied with

Windsor & Newtons 're-touching varnish'. Leave the article to dry and harden in a warmish room. I would advise a little practice first on something that does not matter very much.

Prisoner-of-war Work

Straw Work

This work, though sadly neglected for many years, has now become popular and is certainly worth looking for. Coloured straw as an inlay was never very popular in England – Tunbridge marquetry probably taking its place. But in eighteenth-century France and Holland it was frequently used for this purpose by cabinet-makers. In December 1782 the *Journal de France* announced a sale of furniture at the Hôtel Bullion which included corner cupboards and bureaux inlaid with straw marquetry arranged in floral designs. Floral designs were actually much more the province of the Dutch, who made very clever flower pictures in inlaid straw, while the French excelled in scenic effects.

When, during the Napoleonic Wars, French and Dutch prisoners-of-war were accommodated in British prisons, those among them who were 'pressed' men and had been cabinet makers by trade, got to work, wherever a prison market was allowed, to make objects of straw-inlay work, as well as the rough deal carcases needed as a base. The objects thus made by these prisoners were numerous, cabinets for jewel-cases being the most beautiful. There is a picture on the outside as well as the inside of the lid, and very often on the back, front and sides as well. Inside, the jewel-casket is even more lovely. There are several little compartments, each with a lid, and every one of them inlaid with straw work in glowing colours. The lid to each box is raised by a little tab of silk ribbon, now very frayed, or completely worn away. Work-boxes were provided with small compartments, and very often with a built-in pincushion. A piece of old Vauxhall mirror-glass was often fitted into the lid (Plate 9). Besides jewel- and work-boxes there were such things as embroidery-silk holders, round and oval small boxes, knitting-needle cases, tea caddies, Noah's arks, miniature furniture, children's roll-top desks, fans and face screens.

The carcases in very early straw work were made of thick cardboard, wood at this time not being obtainable, and the straw, undyed, achieved a coloured effect by the way it was laid (Plate 9). Most boxes were lined (when not straw-inlaid) with pink or blue paper. Sometimes the customer who had ordered the box would supply brass locks and hinges, otherwise they were made from any odd bit of metal, and consequently appear clumsy and amateurish. There used to be romantic stories of how the poor prisoners used straw from their mattresses for this work, and boiled bits of coloured rag to obtain the dyes, but according to diaries and records of the time this was not so. Straw was a common commodity in those days and as to the dyes, ribbon, coloured paper, Vauxhall glass, etc, these were supplied readily by the customers who ordered the goods.

There were other prisoner-of-war workers in straw beside the cabinet makers – those who had been hat makers in the days before the war. Fine straw hats were made from very fine plaited straw, the French straw being split far more finely than that of English straw-workers, because the French had invented a straw-splitter that could split one straw into from four to seven strands. But the only relic left of these straw-workers are the 'treen straw-splitters', which were said to have been copied by English hatters and 'let out' to the cottage straw-plaiters by the manufacturers in the hat-making districts. These small relics are very rare, but there is still a possibility of their being discovered.

Refurbishing Straw Inlay   Any straw inlay which has been exposed to strong light will have faded to a uniform brown, and the outside of a casket or work-box will often look most dull and uninteresting; also it will be found that some of the inlay is missing. This is where an informed searcher can find a treasure. Do not be put off by the dreary look of the outside of the box, but lift the lid and look inside. Sunlight and dust will not have entered here, and the inside will be as fresh and glowing as the day it was made. The hinges may need renewing, but this is not a difficult job, and the worn-out silk ribbon tabs can be replaced by fresh pieces of old nineteenth-century ribbon. The top should be freshened up by washing gently with a cloth rung out of warm soap and water. Dry carefully, and then give a light coat of clear picture varnish. This will 'set' any loose pieces of straw and will give a bright look to the faded top, and even to the bare spots of old pine from where the inlay has disappeared altogether. Straw-work is rare, and any piece, however small, is worth finding and rejuvenating.

Bone Work

Among the prisoners-of-war there were also men who were trained in ivory- and bone-carving, mainly from the factories near Dieppe. During their imprisonment they carved astonishingly beautiful caskets and many other things, from the bones obtained from the prison kitchens. There has been a rising market for any of these things that may come up for sale from time to time. Being made of bone they have withstood the onslaught of time remarkably well; and anyone who visits Peterborough Museum which has a very large collection of authentic articles made a few miles away at Norman Cross Prison, will be astonished by the inventiveness of the carvers.

At the top of the list come the wonderful ship models, and working models such as guillotines, ladies spinning, rocking babies, acrobats and many other fascinating things. But these all fetch top prices, and I do not think there has been much left undiscovered in this direction. Occasionally one can come across a bone games-box which holds large sets of dominoes and a few dice. The top usually consists of some form of cribbage-board. These can be highly elaborate with painted lids (Plate 10). Apart from these, easier things to find are cheese or apple scoops made from knuckle bones (Plate 11), pastry-wheels on bone handles and tobacco stoppers in the form of ladies' legs.

All that is needed to clean bone work is soap and water, with a final polish with a white cream; but be sure the cream is removed from any carving by brushing with a soft brush.

7 Miscellaneous Antiques

Miniature Houses

One of my most delightful discoveries has been an early eighteenth-century doll's house. We hear and read a good deal about dolls and dolls' houses these days; the fashion for them has attained such proportions that the date of them almost does not matter at all. No hard-and-fast rule of being over a hundred years old is kept here, and very large prices have been obtained at the leading salerooms for quite recent pieces.

It is perhaps not generally known that the fashion for these miniature houses started at the end of the seventeenth century. At first they were called 'baby houses', and were the outcome of the Dutch shallow, bow-fronted wall cupboards, glazed at the sides as well as the front. At this time there was a craze for anything miniature. Everyone who could afford to do so started to collect such things, and naturally something was needed in which to place these treasures so that they might be shown off to their best advantage. The Dutch glazed cupboards which had a couple of shelves were ideal for these collections of small silver, porcelain, glass, pewter and brass objects. The English, however, preferred to have miniature houses in which to keep their collections of miniatures. Sometimes these houses were copies of the ones they lived in themselves. It is said that Chippendale himself made small copies of the furniture he had supplied for some of these mansions.

It is possible for us to see some of these treasures today, not only in the houses for which they were made, but in museums in various parts of the country. The Bethnal Green Museum in London has a good collection of eighteenth-century dolls' houses containing not only the original furniture, but all the necessary furnishings that make a house complete. And the museum at Tunbridge Wells has a fascinating collection of later ones, and has thoughtfully supplied small movable platforms for very young children to stand on, so that they can peer into the windows of the upper rooms, having first turned down a switch at the side of the house so that every room is illuminated.

It has always been my ambition to find an early dolls' house, though they are so rare I never expected to do so. We have occasionally had the Dutch wall cupboards which were used as such, and I am always looking out for the early English ones. My patience and vigilance were rewarded recently when I spied, hanging on the wall at the back of a stand, at a well-known antiques fair, a wall cupboard with a very pretty central domed top. It did not strike me as being of Dutch manufacture,

F

as the proportions were all wrong for such a piece. It was too deep from back to front, and not high or broad enough. It puzzled me, and I went up to it to get a closer view. It proved to be of oak, with the front, and practically the whole of the sides, glazed, and there were two shelves, which were full to overflowing with a fascinating herd of pottery 'cow-creamers'. The inside appeared to be covered with some shiny dark-brown substance. I asked to be told more about it as it was a most unusual piece and, to my astonishment and delight, was informed that although, being papered over inside, one could not see it from the front, there was a door at the back with lovely iron butterfly hinges. Very diffidently I asked if I could possibly see it off the wall, and in a very short time the cows had been put somewhere else to graze, so that I was able to examine the whole thing thoroughly. There was a large door at the back, which could not be opened because of the inside paper. I bought it without hesitation, but had to wait patiently for the carriers to bring it, as it was too big to go in the car.

When it arrived we started to remove the thick paper, varnished dark brown, with which it was lined. This was a difficult job because we were working through a narrow glass door in the front panel, and were terrified of breaking the original glass. At last we managed to get the top layer off and were then able to open the door at the back which gave us more room to operate. This top paper had obscured a white-washed ceiling, and the moulded frieze at the top of the back and sides. One of the shelves was pine and was warped, and was obviously not original for it was nailed into place instead of resting on supports. We removed both that and the original shelf, and proceeded to remove the rest of the paper layer by layer by damping it slightly. We discovered that there were four other papers, a modern yellow one, a Victorian red-flock one, a green and white one, and finally the original one, of which there was only a few inches left. It was a pity there was not more of it because it was a very early wallpaper, white, with small green sprigs. The inside 'walls' and the one shelf, were now a lighter oak than the outside, but looked very satisfactory when given a good waxing, and the dolls' house was as it had been when it was first made (Plate 11). The domed top had a thick paper label pasted on the outside, which appeared to have something written on it – probably the history of the house – but this was covered with the patina and dirt of ages, and any writing which may have been there was totally undecipherable.

Although the house was supplied with a means of hanging, since holes were bored in the top of the two backboards supporting the door, it was really intended to stand on a table. These tables stood on a landing, or in a gallery, a little away from the wall, and easily moved away from it if any fresh acquisitions had to be placed inside it through the door in the back. The narrow door in the front had been made to open at some time, but I do not think it had originally done so. A great many of the tiny treasures kept in these 'baby houses' were extremely valuable, being 'toys' for adults, and not meant to be played with by children; hence the back door that would remove any such easy temptation. The fashion waned eventually, and the 'baby houses' were removed to the nursery where they immediately became 'dolls' houses', furniture and furnishings for which could be obtained from the toy shops, who were themselves supplied by those who made the individual items. Cheap dolls' house furniture came from Germany later.

The prettiest miniature house I have seen is one I kept myself for my own enjoyment. It is an exact model of a Regency 'Gothic' lodge and I am sure it must have been called The Hermitage. The actual size of the house is 6in across, 4in deep and 5in high. The most outstanding thing about it is that the edifice itself and the garden walls, etc, are made almost entirely of natural coloured cork; the exception being the roof which is painted a soft browny-red with the 'tiles' neatly drawn on it. The material here appears to be a thin cardboard, which also forms the roofs of the two porches, and the two doors beneath them. The ridge on the roof is made of cork. The front has a red door with a Gothic porch and a 'stone' doorstep. There are four front latticed windows, the latticed effect having been achieved by a coarse black net being stretched diagonally across the back of the glass, giving a diamond effect. Behind this are fine hand-made lace curtains. The eave in the roof in front is 'beamed'; this also has a cork ridge. The left end of the house contains the back door with a small red porch supported by cork side-brackets, and there are two latticed windows, one above the other. Jutting out from the end of the house is a small battlemented flat-roofed outhouse; on the end of this is a water-butt. There are no windows at the back of the house, but two tall chimney breasts: one is supplied with two chimney pots, and the other at the kitchen end has one. Next door to this is a small, roofed built-out part, rather like a dog kennel, which is presumably the outside of the bread oven. The other end of the house is very grand. The upper storey, which projects over the ground floor, is supported by beam ends, and contains a large oriel window, with four pointed panes. Over them, immediately beneath the gable, is some sort of carving. The whole of this end is 'beamed', the beams being made of thin strips of brown cardboard. There is a wide latticed window on the ground floor with four panes.

Joining on to the house and extending outwards, is a wall, intended to look like part of a'ruin'; this contains an arched doorway which is filled by an ecclesiastical-looking door. In the wall over the door is a niche containing a figure. In the side garden, under the window, is a row of pink and blue flowers, with a tree at either end with small yellow blossoms on them. A distinctly Regency look is given by the trees and low hedges being composed of small feathers cut to the right shape, and dyed a yellowish green, and the small rockery on either side of the front porch is formed with tiny seashells, which also border the side pathway. The ground is of plain cork, but the pathway from the back door to the shed looks like a piece of flattened plaited straw (Plate 14). The patience that was needed to make anything so tiny, yet so exactly to scale in such materials is phenomenal.

I doubt whether another such cork house exists to be discovered, but pictures made of cork can certainly be found. Cork came prominently into use in the early nineteenth century. Life-jackets, belts and floats for fishing nets were made of it, and therefore any work done in this medium is usually attributed to seamen or fishermen. Some of it undoubtedly was their work, but certainly not all of it. Cork is the outer bark of the cork-oak trees which grow in Portugal, and Portuguese craftsmen made some very fine cork pictures of outdoor scenes, making good use of finely granulated cork for the foliage of trees and bushes. But though these are marvels of good workmanship, to my mind cork is more suitable for making pictures in relief of stone buildings. I had a pair of such pictures years ago depicting Conway and Windsor castles. Strips of cork were cleverly built up on top of each other to give the right effect of stonework. These pictures were about 15in × 12in in size, and had been framed originally in broad gold frames, which some misguided person had painted black. I have found one or two other cork pictures since then, but not of such fine workmanship. Care should be taken to make sure that any cork pictures you buy should be British or Portuguese. Very charming cork pictures are at present being made in Japan, the frame forming part of the picture. These are signed on the back in Japanese characters. They are original, but not, of course, antique.

Cork was supplied in two kinds: 'slab' for buildings, 'granulated' for foliage. The craftswomen in Victorian days must have been able to buy it cut in 'layers' of various thicknesses, so that it could be used to 'build up' for depth, etc. It was probably sold in the art centres and bazaars with other 'craft' materials, such as wax components for flower making, and the tiny objects that were put on the trays held by 'pedlar dolls', as well as the sheets of gold and coloured papers which were used for the lining of boxes and box-frames.

I found two other model houses a few years ago. These were made of thin wood. The outsides were painted to represent houses, of which the insides were fitted up as work-boxes which were revealed when the roof was taken off. There were also drawers in the base for sewing implements, cleverly disguised as steps, etc. The period was about 1810–15 and they were exceedingly attractive. Another fine wooden model we had was an exact replica of a Kentish oast house. It was enchantingly complete down to a small figure of a miller dressed in authentic clothes, and there were two beautiful little sacks of hops waiting outside to be picked up.

I should very much have liked to keep all these house models, but one of the drawbacks of being an antique dealer is that it is certainly not possible to keep all the fascinating things one finds, otherwise there would be no stock! So I part from them with great regret, having hung on to them as long as possible, and I am very glad if I know they are going to good homes!

Miniature Brass Furniture

This can still be discovered if one searches hard enough for it. I know this to be true, for I collect it myself. It has taken years to gather a small collection, probably because I am fussy and prefer to have everything to a certain scale – that of doll's house furniture – and I prefer it to be of the Georgian or early Victorian periods. But if anyone is thinking of starting such a collection, I will say at once that though the price is reasonable, such miniature furniture is not always easy to find.

These attractive little pieces were made, not so much as toys for children to play with, but as mantelpiece ornaments. Some things were, of course, made to furnish dolls' houses – the kind of thing one would expect to find made of brass in one's own home – candlesticks, hearth furniture, etc. They were made by the small brass-manufacturers of Birmingham, who worked in their own homes having bought sheet brass from the larger firms to make such things as shoe and belt buckles and the smaller buckles for fastening the knees of breeches – such things being necessities for the clothes of the eighteenth century. But fashions change, and at the beginning of the nineteenth century shoe buckles went out for the élite because new-fangled laces had been introduced for men's shoes, and heel-less slippers with no ornament at all for women. The manufacturers faced bankruptcy, and appealed to the Prince Regent to continue to wear buckled shoes in order to keep them in fashion. It is recorded that, although he did so, the élite preferred the new ideas and showed no intention of following his example. So the small brass-manufacturer had to turn his attention to other directions in order to save his business. Mantelpiece ornaments in the form of flat brass figures, was the result. They were made in pairs such as 'Robinson Crusoe and Man Friday', 'The Gamekeeper and the Poacher', and groups of exotic birds, such as it was fashionable to keep in aviaries at that time. Small tip-up tripod tables, hearth furniture and candlesticks followed and, later in the nineteenth century, more furniture and other things were made, but in a larger size, too big to go in a doll's house.

My collection of small brass furniture consisting of 3 tripod tables, 5 late Georgian chairs, 1 rocking chair, fire-irons and fender, trivets both high and low, a smoothing iron, a pair of small steps, a folding towel rail, 2 tiny pairs of eighteenth-century candlesticks, and a pestle and mortar about an inch high. Later period pieces are a mangle with wooden rollers, a luggage trolley and a wheelbarrow. To my ever-lasting regret I parted with a cradle and a chest-of-drawers with pewter knobs – really a money box – before I started collecting in earnest for myself. I have a small bell-metal hob-grate made specially for a doll's house, and not a traveller's sample because, unlike these last, it has no standing base, and has to be fixed to the wall. The collection fascinates everyone who sees it, especially the men!

Love Tokens

Treen

I often wonder why people do not concentrate solely on making a collection of these endearing objects. Most of them are small and take up little room, and though some of them are perhaps expensive, others are very reasonably priced. But one must know all about what one is looking for, otherwise many things will go undiscovered or be passed by because, being small, they are often stowed away with jewellery and other *objet d'arts* in glass-fronted showcases or cabinets. A great many love tokens were made of wood, and come under the heading of 'treen'. The largest number were made by the Welsh, but they were made in other parts of Britain as well as in Europe.

Under the heading of treen, objects made for the loved ones included spoons, knitting sheaths, snuff-boxes, needle-cases, lace bobbins, stay-busks and just plain amulets. A love token can always be distinguished by the 'heart' which is invariably carved, or inlaid, in the material it is made of. There is also a flower with four petals shaped like commas which means the 'soul', and a wheel which means 'I will work for you'. All the things enumerated above are carved in some way or other, some of them very elaborately. Sometimes they have names, or initials, and a date carved on them. An amulet we have just acquired in the shape of a heart incorporates the wheel in the carving, and bears one of the earliest dates known on love tokens – 1641 (Plate 12).

Spoons and stay-busks These examples of treen are the most expensive, and the latter the most difficult to find. The spoons are now being reproduced, and might take in the inexperienced. Knitting sheaths – except for those that are very beautifully carved – are reasonable in price. There are two main types of these: variants of a straight shape to be anchored in a belt or apron strap; and what is known as the 'goose-wing' shape, for use under the arm. A great many of these come from the north of England where they were extensively used by both men and women alike. There will have been no time spent in decorative carving, but a choice wood such as yew-tree will have been chosen for the making, and the initials of the owner imprinted in some way, sometimes even with small brass nails. The object of the knitting sheath was to hold the needle so that it was only necessary to 'throw' the wool. This left one hand free to use in emergencies, without having to put the knitting down (Plate 13).

Lace Bobbins (Plate 13) Carved wooden ones are rare, and the plain turned ones would not have been considered good enough to use as love tokens; but ivory or bone bobbins used for making Buckinghamshire lace were given, with names and dates and often an encouraging phrase such as 'Come kiss me quick'! inscribed with dots diagonally between coloured lines. These are intensively collected, but by dint of examining the interior of old work-boxes, etc, the searcher might find himself rewarded.

Shoe Snuff-boxes (Plate 15) These, especially if made in the shape of a shoe (which meant 'good luck') were special favourites as love tokens. Usually they are highly expensive. Some also were made to order for special customers by French prisoners-of-war, during the Napoleonic Wars. These were often made as a pair of shoes joined together and contained a set of miniscule dominoes where one would expect to find the snuff. Snuff-shoes made in England were models of real shoes, and were probably made by the last-maker. The soles and heels had tiny brass nails all round them, and brass ornamentations on the uppers were made with the same kind of nails. One sometimes finds the word 'love' impressed with them on the draw-out lid on the shoe's top. Some very rare wooden snuff-boxes were made in the form of bellows about 3in long. These also were decorated with small brass nails, and 'I love you' or 'my only love' was the message inscribed on the front of the bellows. The back pulled out.

Brass Love Tokens

These are not so common as the wooden ones, but do exist, mainly in the form of snuff-boxes inlaid with a copper heart or initial. Brass knitting sheaths were made in the north of England, but these are very rare. Odd smallish pieces in brass that could be used in everyday life by the loved one are sometimes found, such as iron-stands in the shape of a heart, or with a pierced heart in the middle, and brass toasting-forks with a heart at the top of the handle to suspend it by. We have also had brass or steel trivets in the form of a heart, or with a heart incorporated in the ornamentation.

Shells

Shell 'Valentines' were bought ready-made in Barbados and brought back home by the sailors for their sweethearts and wives. They consisted of glass-covered round boxes, with coloured shells arranged geometrically inside (Plate 12). In the same category as 'sailors' love-tokens' we can place the scrimshaw work done on the whaling ships by sailors using whale tusks or teeth. Drinking vessels could be made from the thicker ends, and the tips were used mainly for ornaments. Whale bones were turned into stay-busks. The method used for doing this scrimshaw work was to scratch or score a deep design on the ivory, and then to rub in a reddish-brown colouring matter, so that the design stood out. Modern scrimshaw work is being done now, but it all looks very new. The colouring matter is bright, instead of being almost black with age, and whereas all kinds of odd designs were used in by-gone days, the modern ones all appear to be of hunting scenes, and the work done mainly on drinking mugs.

Plate 13 (*above*) A selection of knitting sheaths. From left to right: 'goose-wing' shape made out of one piece of walnut, a simply carved one of boxwood, a round one of carved boxwood with brass-mounted top, an early one of oak and a very simple type in fruit-wood; (*below*) an assortment of finely-turned wooden lace bobbins, decorated with brass-wire or pewter bands

Plate 14 (*above*) Bookmarker of silk. The lettering is embroidered by machinery; (*below*) miniature house made of cork. It measures 6in across, 4in from back to front, and is 5in high. The trees are made of feathers and the rockeries of tiny shells

Plate 15 (*above*) Shoe snuff-boxes made in the early nineteenth century of wood, probably by the last-maker. The leather high-shoe in the middle is a model on its own wooden last; (*below*) horse brasses on leathers which fitted over the ends of brass 'hames'. These were made for a pair of shire horses on a Cotswold farm

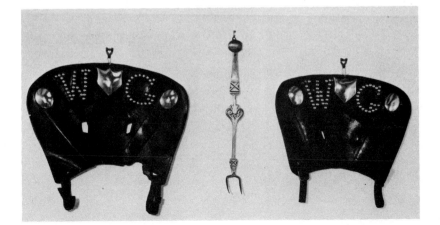

Plate 16   (*above*) Early French copper weather-vane. The bird was made 'in the round', not cut out of the flat; (*below*) royal coat-of-arms in bronze. Probably from a pediment on a gateway of one of the royal parks

Horn

This is a material in some way akin to ivory. Sheep horns were used for snuff-mills and powder-flasks, mugs could be cut from the horns of big cattle. Horn spoons can also be found. The mugs and horns are etched in the same way as whalebone. The snuff-mills and powder horns might be silver-mounted. Combs were made from horn – high Spanish combs and side combs, as well as the ordinary kind – and I have seen rather late dark horn spoons silver-mounted as 'christening' spoons, which one might say was another form of love token. As general guidance in dating objects made of horn, the honey coloured, and the brown and cream horn was earlier than the black and white horn. Horn was used for the manufacture of many things right through the ages until the invention of plastics, and the trade of 'horner' was an old and an honourable one.

Glass

One sees many beautifully etched glasses intended as love tokens, or given as wedding presents, but this is rather straying into another subject. The only true 'folk' love token made of glass, was the hollow glass rolling-pin in bright colours, sometimes with a picture of a ship painted on it. It was corked at one end, and is said to have had various uses; one that it was meant to be filled with cold water to keep the hands cool while pastry-making, another that it had originally been filled with illicit brandy. But whatever the story, it usually ended up by having a ribbon attached to either end of the pin to form a loop from which it could be suspended in the window, where it looked very pretty both from inside and out – and possibly aroused feelings of envy in the breasts of the girls who had not been the recipient.

Valentines

The Victorian kind of Valentine with a lacy edge and very senti-mental words on it turns up from time to time, and some should be included in any collection of love tokens, for what could be more of a message of love than this? The place to look for them is on second-hand book stalls among collections of old Christmas cards, or in old scrap albums. The subject of albums reminds me that years ago when I first had my shop in St Christopher's Place, London, I undertook a job for one of my customers, namely to catalogue his collection of bookmarkers, and stitch them carefully into an album. They could not be stuck in, in case they had to be rearranged at some future time.

When finished, the album was presented to the Victoria and Albert Museum. He was a keen collector of papier-mâché, and most of it was given to the museum, where it can be seen in the rooms devoted to Victorian furniture. It was this gentleman who first suggested I should write a book on the subject of papier-mâché.

Bookmarkers

These were undoubtedly given as love tokens. But I had not realised until I started sorting them out and arranging them, how many different types there are. They include cross stitch in wool on canvas, cross stitch in silk on taffetas, embroidered silk in various designs such as Faith, Hope and Charity (a cross, anchor and heart), words of secular birthday greetings in verse form, or scriptural texts. There were even markers worked in silk on paper canvas – on which one would have to be careful not to make a wrong stitch, because the paper would tear if any attempt at unpicking stitches was made.

All these bookmarkers were backed with brightly coloured silk ribbon in shades of purple, red or blue, that were twice as long as the canvas. Sometimes the ends of the ribbon which hung outside the book were fringed, sometimes turned in like a 'V' at the bottom, and a tassel or Venetian bead sewn on to the point (Plate 14). The Coventry firm of Stevens made bookmarkers as well as the better-known 'Stevengraphs'. For some reason or other the former have never soared in price like the latter have done, and can still be obtained at a reasonable sum.

The best place to find these various bookmarkers is in large family Bibles, or volumes of Shakespeare's works, and certainly the best way of showing them off is to stitch them into albums.

Silk Pincushions

It may seem strange to give pincushions as love tokens but it must be remembered that pins were once quite valuable things and for a long time, before buttons were invented, were one of the main ways of fastening garments. Indeed rather grand editions are still used today to fasten such things as stocks, cravats, scarves, plaids, etc. Pins were not cheap because they were difficult to make; hence the phrase 'pin money', and the saying 'See a pin and pick it up, all the day you'll have good luck.' As pins were expensive commodities, they had to be carefully preserved when not actually in use, and this was done by making cushions into which they could be stuck.

Early pincushions were round soft balls of cotton-wool covered with embroidery, from which a ribbon depended so that they could be hung from the waist-belt. There were larger ones to go on a dressing-table, and smaller editions were made for work-boxes. These were filled with cotton-wool made from the waste of flax or silk, sawdust, or, as a protection against rust, emery powder. Those made as love tokens were shaped like a heart. The outer cover was of silk, possibly with a lace frill round it and, spelt out in pins pushed firmly into the cushion, was a phrase like 'I love you'. Pincushions were also made for the layette basket as a gift to the expected baby. I had a very elaborate silk and lace one once on which the pin message was 'Welcome, little stranger'.

Pincushions made in the shape of hearts were quite common up to World War I. I saw one in a local antiques fair the other day, obviously made by a soldier out of odds and ends of ceremonial uniform. The date was somewhere round about 1920; the loving message still spelt out in pins.

8 Antique Metals

I intend here to deal only with ordinary metals. The valuable ones must be classed with early pottery, porcelain, glass and jewellery; such things are not easily disguised, except by dirt, and there are very many knowledgeable people interested in them, which considerably lessens the chances of finding them. Antiques made of ordinary metals are not only disguised by dirt, but by buffing, brazing, acid-washing and lacquering, which means that nearly everything from late seventeenth-century candlesticks to articles made in the late Victorian period, will all look exactly the same – brighter than bright. It will need a very astute or lucky person to be able to make a worthwhile discovery, for not only does a metal look much the same, whatever its age, but there is an acute shortage of antique metal of any kind. This started during World War II, when there were 'salvage drives' for metals of all kinds, and many willing sacrifices were made. Sometimes the sacrifice was in vain. There was one humorously pathetic story of a friend of mine who sacrificed her cherished set of aluminium pans, and then went out to buy something to replace them made of a material less essential to the war effort – and all she could find were brand-new sets of aluminium cooking pans!

Antique wrought-iron gates proved to be of no use, so these were sold to dealers in such things. And, before the owners realised that pewter was not wanted as salvage, large quantities of antique pewter had been put in the salvage carts, and arrived at the depots too scratched and battered to be of use to anyone. After the war was over there was understandably a shortage of copper and brass; but then the price of copper suddenly rose until it was a much better proposition to sell it to the scrap-metal merchants than to the antique dealers, so much of what was old and valuable was lost for ever. However, there was still a reasonable amount of antique brass and pewter articles remaining at reasonable prices until, after a year or two, Dutch dealers realising this, and anxious to replace all that had been taken away from them during the war by the Germans, started coming over here to buy – pewter, brass and Delft being their chief requirements. Since then the supply of pewter has been gradually drained out of the country, so that it has almost reached zero level.

The Dutch were not the only overseas buyers however. Americans were now very keen to purchase pewter tankards. Before the war they had not been much interested, but during the war American troops stationed in England got used to drinking beer out of pewter tankards and many of them took a few home with them. Very soon not only tankards were being exported, but all other pewter ware as well.

Pewter and Britannia Metal

English collectors were now turning their attention to the early pewter pieces, and anyone who acquired an oak dresser was buying pewter dishes, platters and chargers with which to 'dress' the shelves. In fact there was such a demand for pewter that reproductions were made to satisfy it, and some metal manufacturers started to buy up all the Britannia metal they could find with the idea of melting it down to make 'pewter'. So the market was flooded with rather dead-looking tankards, measures, candlesticks and very small plates made of this substance but which were very close copies of the genuine pewter originals. Consequently Britannia metal also has now almost completely disappeared from the market, which is a pity because it had a certain value in its own right.

When it was first invented in the late eighteenth century, it was known as the 'poor man's Sheffield plate'. The main difference is that Sheffield plate (see page 112) is composed of silver fused on copper, whereas Britannia metal has for its base an inferior type of pewter – the constituents of this being the same as in better pewter but the quantities varying. To compare the two would be rather like comparing skimmed milk with cream. Silver was very thinly plated over this base, but the article looked almost as good as Sheffield plate when it was new. Only smallish objects were made, such as tea-pots, cream jugs, sugar bowls, egg cups and the lids to pottery hot-water jugs. Early Britannia metal was well modelled; a few of the small tea-pots made at that time, now having lost the silver plating, are found labelled as 'pewter'. Later, a cheaper and thinner metal base was made, highly engraved and chased; but the silver, being more thinly plated than ever, wore off very quickly revealing the pewter-looking body underneath, and this came to be sold as genuine pewter by inexpert dealers.

Brass

Articles made of this metal still remained in fairly good supply until a few years ago. Then the sudden jump into fashion of oak furniture meant that there was an equally sudden demand for brass candlesticks, toasting forks, chestnut-roasters, basting-spoons, ladles and strainers. All such things should be well examined before buying, for this reason that, about twenty years ago, a well-known reputable firm was making extremely good reproductions of all of them. Now, with two decades of wear and polish, they have acquired such an antique 'patina' that the less knowledgeable collector might be pardoned for mistaking them for originals, and recently clever Japanese craftsmen have been turning their attention to making copies of the late seventeenth- and early eighteenth-century candlesticks. True they have the word 'Japan' impressed on them in some rather unnoticeable spot, but this mark can be removed with a sharp instrument. The resultant scar is apparent to the vigilant, but the less wary might be deceived. Brass and copper warming-pans are being reproduced, but they are very obvious copies, and the inferior quality of the turned wood handles gives them away at once.

At the moment of writing, there is a limited amount buyable of genuine brass or bell-metal pestles and mortars, skillets, jammers, pans, kettles and measures. Take care with mortars, several of these have been made out of empty shell-cases used in the war.

Horse Brasses

These have always been popular things to collect but it should be remembered that three distinct kinds may be disguised by dirt and discolouration:

1   The really old ones, with or without leathers.
2   Those being made at the present time to decorate working horses on show days. These are well-made, and are stocked by the saddler, who will also supply any leathers needed.
3   Fakes, made of thin, roughly-finished brass, either singly or attached to cheap-looking leather. These are made for the tourist-trade shops. The unfortunate thing is that they turn up from time-to-time in house sales and other places. Having acquired a certain amount of dirt they might, to the untutored eye, be taken for the real thing.

Genuine old horse brasses are really lovely, being made of solid good-coloured brass, often attached to the original stout leather straps or other harness. The leather is thick, and greasy at the back with wear, but well polished in front. They will not be cheap, nor as the saying goes 'readily available'. The history of these brasses is fascinating: originally they were worn as amulets or charms against bad luck, or as talismans to bring good luck to the horse's owner. Among old brasses we find: acorns, Prince-of-Wales feathers, roses, shamrocks, thistles, stars, moons, suns, hearts, diamonds, clubs, horses (rampant and running), stags, ships and, later on, steam engines. Other horse brasses commemorating events have been made too (Plate 15).

Copper

Articles of copper were chiefly made for domestic use until the twentieth century; therefore we look for such things as copper measures, tun-dishes, kettles and pans, warming-pans, beer-warmers, both boot-shaped and conical, scuttles, and the large round coffers used for boiling clothes in before the advent of washing machines. Anything copper used for cooking (with the exception of jammers) had to be tinned on the inside to avoid the danger of copper poisoning. Practically all these things are very simple and ordinary in shape. It was not until the coming of art nouveau in the 1890s that copper articles were made for the sitting-room, such as fenders, refined scuttles, fire-irons, trays and small ash-trays.

In late Victorian and Edwardian days flowers were arranged very simply in silver or cut-glass vases, and plants were placed in coloured earthenware pots. But since flower arranging became a cult, more and more people are looking for suitable antique receptacles for their flower arrangements. Wood has become popular, small things like tea-caddies and knife-boxes, and larger things such as cradles, being used. There is, however, a nucleus of flower arrangers who prefer copper receptacles. But they do not want ordinary domestic 'kitchen-stuff', and insist that copper vessels are obtainable in pretty shapes more suitable for living-rooms. I discovered what they meant when I found a beautiful Sheffield-plate cream jug, from which all the silver had disappeared. Naturally it looked like copper because it was copper, but it had not started life as such, being the cream jug in a tea-set made of a much superior metal.

Sheffield Plate

This beautiful metal, already mentioned, was made of silver fused on copper, and in pristine condition it is considered the equal, in antique value, of its silver counterpart. But when the silver has worn off through constant polishing and wear, it can be bought quite reasonably, and such things as cream jugs, tankards, bowls, coasters, and chamber-candlesticks with deep saucers, do make very charming receptacles for flowers. Traces of silver will be found on old Sheffield plate, especially on the base. But the piece can be cleaned in exactly the same way as copper.

Tin

Articles made of this metal go very well with, or as substitute for, pewter. Tin candlesticks were made in all sizes, to hold the tallow candles made for use in the domestic parts of big houses, cottages and ships. They are usually made with a slide to push up the candle as it burns away, operated by a button or key at the side. I recently saw in an antique shop what I thought to be a large tin jug of an eighteenth-century shape. This was unusual because tin vessels such as jugs or mugs were of much later date. But then I noticed on the sides, which would have received more polish than the rest of the jug, gleams of lovely glowing copper. The result was unusual but delightful. I was assured that the jug was of copper, tinned on the outside. The owner and I both came to the conclusion that a pewter collector had had it tinned because he wanted a jug of that shape to go with his collection, perhaps to hang up on a dresser, therefore the usual process was reversed and the outside was tinned instead of the inside.

Steel

Smallish articles made of steel are uncommon, and certainly worth searching for, as early steel objects can be valuable. Eighteenth-century snuff-boxes and snuff-rasps, as well as shoe buckles, would be delightful things to find. The workmanship of such things is superb. There was also a certain amount of cut-steel jewellery made – small buckles, brooches, muff-chains and châtelaines for instance. Early steel implements made specially for work-boxes and etuis can in themselves form an interesting and fascinating collection.

Many years ago we attended a sale of the private collection of a doctor at Enfield, which included some treen. The treen was interesting, and we were able to buy some, but even more interesting was his collection of early steel pieces such as those already mentioned. Included in the collection was a large oval steel belt, about 2–3in wide with a hinge at one side and a padlock at the other. It was beautifully engraved with an English name and an eighteenth-century date. We had an idea it had originally been made as a belt for one of the little 'blackamoors', so fashionable as ladies' pages at that time, however, search though we might, we could find no reference to such a thing having been made. But as the name of the manufacturer was impressed on one end of the belt we made inquiries and found that the firm still existed and were now famous for the manufacture of handcuffs and steel locks and keys, etc. Their place of business had been bombed out in London and they were then at Newbury in Berkshire. We wrote to them, giving a description of the belt, and asked if they could tell us anything about it. We received a prompt reply saying that although they had been bombed out of their London premises and many of their records had perished, they could tell us that what we possessed was not a belt at all, but a camel collar, one of several made to the order of the man named on it. He was a wealthy merchant with a string of camels in Egypt, which were used to transport his merchandise across the desert to the nearest port for England. How or why this particular collar got over here, we were never able to discover.

Iron

Anything genuinely antique in wrought or moulded iron is sure to be attractive. Georgian and Victorian boot-scrapers are both useful and ornamental; so are Victorian iron door-stops and umbrella stands. One must have a good knowledge of this subject, because all these things are being reproduced, and not only reproduced, but old ones are now given a hard bright 'armour-steel' finish so that one cannot tell 't'other from which'. But out-of-the-way iron articles can be found occasionally although their purpose is not always apparent.

Years ago I bought a large crucifix in moulded iron. The cross was set on the top of a short flight of steps so that it stood steady. I could not understand for what purpose such a thing could have been made; it was quite certainly antique, but one could not imagine it standing on an altar. I had only paid a few shillings for it but was determined to try and find out something about its history. Having searched all the text books in vain I took it, as I thought, to the ultimate authority, a gentleman who eyed it with a kind of supercilious horror, and then told me it was not valuable. I answered that I was quite aware of that, but just wanted to know for what purpose it had been made. He was unable to tell me. Years afterwards, delving into quite another matter altogether, I came across a picture of an exactly similar iron crucifix. The information given was that they were of eighteenth- and early nineteenth-century origin, and it was the custom at that time to place such pious objects at the foot of a coffin awaiting burial.

Wrought-iron objects such as spoons and other cooking implements, and the lovely racks on which they hang, are being reproduced in Spain. The work is of the highest quality, so much so that it can only too easily be mistaken for old Sussex work.

Metal Objects Used Out-of-doors

These are usually weather-vanes of either wrought iron or copper (Plate 16). Early ones are hard to find, but many were made in the nineteenth and early twentieth centuries which by now have become so weather-beaten that it is difficult to date them with certainty. One should be guided by the kind of subject depicted. An early nineteenth-century one we had was of a farmer in a smock leading a loaded hay-wain, his sheepdog running behind him. At the moment we have an amusing copper vane 'weathering' in the garden, as at some time the owners had had it buffed, so that it looked as if it had been made yesterday. It is the greatest pity to clean away the lovely green patination age has given to copper, and this particular weather-vane would really have looked better as it was, for the subject was pigs rooting about for apples in an orchard.

Other things for out-of-door use were the large iron models of the lion and unicorn which were made to stand above post-office doors. They look well on either side of the front door of a large country house or as fire-dogs in big hearths. It is as well to remember that brand-new editions of these are now being made.

A handsome, but unusual, out-of-door piece is the bronze or iron crest usually found over gateways, or attached to each of the wrought-iron gates themselves. One does not often see such things for sale, but they are certainly worth buying if one has a house big enough to display them. The royal coat-of-arms in Plate 16 is immensely heavy, being made of bronze. It was made in the days of the Georges when the 'white horse of Hanover' was still part of the crest. From the fixings on the back, it had originally been mounted over a gate, probably of one of the Royal Parks. How it came to be offered for sale to the general public is a mystery.

Cleaning Metals

Brass and Copper

Antique brass and copper achieves a lovely mellow colour with age, and should only be cleaned and hand polished by old-fashioned methods. To have it buffed or burnished will destroy its character and value. Lacquering, when necessary, should be done by experts. If the articles are very dirty, immerse them in a bowl or bucket of very hot water to which a generous quantity of detergent has been added. Before the water cools take them out, dry them thoroughly, and while still warm polish with any well-known metal polish; taking care that none of it is left in any cracks or crevices – it can be brushed out with an old nail-brush. If the weather is wet or foggy a final polish with furniture cream helps a little to prevent the articles from tarnishing so quickly.

Copper that has gone green with age should only be polished with furniture cream. It is a pity, as already mentioned, to remove the old patina. One can also treat the outsides of old skillets that have gone dark with being stood in the embers on the hearth in this way. The insides should be kept bright, so polish with metal polish.

If any brass, copper, or tin container needed for flowers is found to have 'sprung a leak' from some hole in the base, a most useful trick is to shave an inch or two from the end of a candle into the article, then stand it on a warm stove or other hot place till the wax is melted. The melted wax will run all over the bottom and form a waterproof cover for the leak. Water only hardens this, and it will last for years. Do not be too sparing with the candle shavings.

Brass Handles   There is a good reason, if the owner prefers antique handles, etc, to be bright, for lacquering such things. Cleaning them when in situation on the furniture with metal polish – unless extremely carefully applied – is sure to leave an unsightly white mark on the wood round the fittings, which is difficult to remove. If the plates to the handles, etc, are of pierced brass, then the metal polish coagulates in the cut-out brasswork and forms a green cake on the wood beneath. I have removed these plates from furniture in order to clean it thoroughly and in bad cases have had to prise them off with a knife, and then had to scrape the thick cake of brass polish deposit away from the woodwork. If cut-work brass plates (and the grips and bolts) are lacquered, this trouble will not occur. Most people use all kinds of polish much too generously and then wonder why it is difficult to get a good polish, or avoid a smeary look afterwards. A golden rule to remember when polishing already well-polished furniture is that the less you put on, the quicker and easier it will be to achieve a high polish.

Tin and Steel

Rust will be the chief trouble here, but luckily there is now a good preparation on the market which will remove it. I believe the same firm also makes a polish which is good for all steel hearth-furniture. If candle-fat remains tightly fixed in old candlesticks it can be removed by steeping in hot water, or placing in a warm oven until it softens enough to remove easily.

Pewter

To clean or not to clean has always been a problem to collectors. My own opinion is that while all very early pewter should certainly be left alone, the domestic kind used for eating and drinking should be kept bright. In the days when this was first made it was cleaned with sand, but this would seem a little drastic nowadays. It can be cleaned, preferably with a metal polish; I do not think silver polish is as good. Spots can be cleaned off with a light application of soapy steel wool – rub the article first with a little oil to avoid scratching. If plates, etc, are corroded, and buffing is needed, it should be done by an expert otherwise all the maker's marks will be buffed away. This will immediately decrease the value.

Iron

Victorian moulded iron such as door-stops, foot-scrapers, etc, should just be washed well with soap and hot water, then polished with black shoe polish. This gives a nice soft effect, which will not come off when handled.

Bell-metal

This is often used for pans, skillets, pestles and mortars – and, of course, bells! It should be polished in the same way as brass. This metal is an alloy of copper and tin, but with more tin than there is in brass, hence the pale almost silvery look.

Culled From an Old Recipe Book of 1823

TO CLEAN TIN COVERS AND PATENT PEWTER PORTER-POTS

Get the finest whiting: mix a little of it
powdered with the least drop of sweet oil, and rub
well and wipe clean: then dust some dry whiting
in a muslin bag over, and rub bright with a dry
leather. The last is to prevent rust.

9 Conservation of Church
Antiques

I feel sure that a true lover of antiques does not set out to make discoveries solely for his own pleasure or gain, but also with the wish to help in any way possible to restore and conserve anything that may be found, for the sake of posterity. But although the average person interested in antiques avidly hunts through salerooms and shops in hopes of finding an unusual treasure, he so seldom seems to think of carefully, albeit reverently, examining the furniture he sees in the less obvious corners of a church. Yet it is here that many undiscovered antiques may still remain but, being undiscovered, in constant danger of being lost for ever. One of my jobs has been the restoration of antique frontals and vestments in some of our old parish churches, and while there I have noticed with pleasure the pieces of beautiful antique furniture the smallest church often contains. It was therefore no surprise to me to read the following account, published in the *Daily Telegraph* in July 1974:

CHAIRS FOUND IN CHURCH WORTH £3,000   By Les Able
Six old walnut ladder-back chairs which have stood almost unnoticed for 65 years in a side chapel of a 12th-century village church have been valued at nearly £3,000. Their value was discovered because of a chance visit by Mr. Simon Jarvis, assistant keeper with the Victoria and Albert Museum, to the Church in Newport, Essex. The chairs, made in about 1750, are thought to be the latest examples of the work of Giles Grandey, the 18th-century furniture maker. One of them has part of the maker's label still intact and has been insured for £800. It is now on semi-permanent loan to the Victoria and Albert Museum. Reseated in rush, it will be on display in the 18th-century English gallery.

Although the church needs anything up to £3,000 to repair stonework in the next few years, Mr. Reginald Humphries, vicar of Newport, is reluctant to sell the chairs to raise money: 'They were probably a gift to the church and I am not happy about making easy money from selling gifts.'

Such a find must have alerted many people to the fact that valuable pieces of furniture, hitherto unnoticed, may be standing in the old church which they attend. Indeed rare and beautiful pieces of furniture may have been put to some mundane use in which they are getting badly damaged. A refectory table used as an altar is well tended and looked after, but I have seen such things used at the backs of churches as receptacles for hymn books and offertory boxes; and old muniment chests pushed away in dark places to hold unwanted flower vases.

Seventeenth-century gate-leg tables are often found in vestries, many of them having been there since the time they were made. If a gate-leg table had been in use in a house all that time it would have been kept polished, but one from a church I saw recently and which was being offered for sale had never had a spot of polish in all its long existence. The beautiful turned legs were so dry that the wood was cracking, and the top, as one would expect, was ink-stained and scratched. This table in a well-kept state would have been valuable, and it seems a pity that such things should be neglected through indifference or ignorance. A polish to the legs every month or so, and a green baize cloth on the top would have kept it in good order in the vestry for another 200 years. We bought a gate-leg table once that had been in the vestry of a very ancient church all its life. The church had been declared redundant and for some time was shut up, until eventually it was turned into a small theatre, and a great deal of rebuilding and renovation was carried out. Evidently the table – a very massive one – had been found very useful during this time, because it took at least a fortnight to remove the whitewash, plaster and even mortar from the legs, and many more weeks to restore the whole of it to its original colour and polish. But it was accomplished and one hopes it may last, if cared for, at least another couple of hundred years.

Chests and coffers, if not neglected, can continue to do the job for which they were made centuries ago. There is, for instance, a fine example of a thirteenth-century oak chest, known as the 'Crusaders' chest' in old Bosham Church near Chichester. It stands against the south wall of the choir and is a lovely mellow oatmeal colour, and so fresh and well preserved that it is difficult to believe it is a medieval relic. Moreover, it is still doing the duty for which it was made 700 years ago, being used as a storage place. It is said that the little fixed box inside at the top has a false bottom, and that in the cavity revealed by its withdrawal was found a silver halfpenny of Edward I's reign. Any museum would be proud to own such a piece, but it is still in the church for any visitor to admire and wonder at. This is by no means the only treasure in this historic Saxon church. The tower was built as a defence against the Danes, and the glorious Saxon arch which divides the chancel from the nave, figures in that part of the Bayeux tapestry which depicts Harold leaving Bosham to go on a visit to Normandy.

In the chancels of most old churches can be found fine examples of seventeenth-century carved oak chairs, for the use of the priest when taking services. And it is by no means unusual to see a joint-stool or two for the use of the servers. These are usually well-kept and polished, but many need an occasional inspection, lest damp or worm should have done any damage, or old pegs be in need of replacement. I am not suggesting that such things should be specially insured against fire or theft; I know only too well that this would be an added burden on a poor parish. All I am asking is that these pieces of furniture should be looked after with the same care they would receive if they were in their custodians' own homes. And I might also make a plea to visitors who have been gifted in any way with a knowledge of repair work and are willing to do so, to offer their help or advice to the vicar, who will doubtless tell them that the needed repairs had been neglected through lack of funds.

It has been mentioned before that a good knowledge of early oak furniture may often lead to the discovery of unsuspected treasures even in places where one would not expect this to happen. Not long ago in Winchester Cathedral a tall medieval cupboard was discovered hidden away in a range of Victorian painted cupboards in which cassocks and surplices were kept for the use of the choir. This discovery was made by an old friend of ours, an antique dealer, who was also responsible for keeping the woodwork of the cathedral in order. He happened to notice the hinges on the cupboard one day. They were early, and not the type usually associated with Victorian cupboards. Further examination proved that it was indeed very much earlier than any of the others. He had it extracted from its Victorian neighbours and the exterior paintwork stripped off. It was then discovered to be a medieval oak book-press. The doors were carved, but in order that the paint should lie smoothly on them, the carving had been filled in with putty till the whole surface was quite flat! Apart from the removal of the paint and putty the piece needed very little restoration. The long iron hinges were now revealed in all their beauty, and luckily the original green paint on the interior of the cupboard had not been touched. It can now be seen in its original condition in one of the chapels in the north transept of the cathedral.

I recently read a very interesting account in the *British Antique Dealers Association Journal* of how two members of the Antiquarian Horological Society discovered an ancient clock in great need of care and attention in a small country church. They would not have discovered the clock at all but for seeing a large notice bearing the words:

This clock was given by the will of Jane Beresford widow, Lady of this Manor: that it may remind all who hear it to spend their time in an honest Discharge of their Calling, and in the Worship of God: that Repentance may not come too late. MDCCLXXII.

The single-handed dial to the clock was on the outside of the tower looking rusty and neglected. The works could not be seen as the door to the tower was locked, but some 5ft of the pendulum shaft with its large iron bob, could be seen hanging motionless below a high opening in the vestry ceiling. The clock had evidently been out of commission for some time, and the two visitors departed feeling rather depressed, for the clock was an early type of about 1720, and rare because of its one hand and very long pendulum – there being very few working examples of these left. They eventually obtained permission to examine the clock more closely, and found that though it was in a neglected state, it was not beyond repair. They then had a meeting with the Lord of the Manor who explained that the clock had been out of action for some years, but there was no money to repair it, as the fabric of the church was in greater need of repair. The visitors then offered to repair the clock at their own expense – an offer which was gratefully accepted.

Some days later the job was begun. With the aid of many willing helpers the clock loft was cleared of all its dirt and debris, due to birds, and the pendulum was released slowly and safely. The clock was dismantled and removed, and the dial taken down from the church tower. All was then taken to a workshop to be examined by a repair team, who came to the conclusion that the clock, because of its historical value, was worthy of complete restoration. The wooden board bearing the clock face was found to be worm-eaten, so was replaced by a new one. Ten months after its removal the clock was returned to its original position, and after a few minor adjustments began working again quite satisfactorily.

This devoted piece of conservation was carried out by two dedicated men at their own expense. I feel sure that there must be many more unrecorded deeds of the same nature, and hope there will be many more to come. Perhaps it might be a good idea for any ancient church open to visitors, to have an offertory box specially for 'The Preservation of the Antique Furnishings of This Church'. There are many antique lovers who would contribute.

I may be asked why poor parishes in need of funds for repair work to the fabric of the church, do not sell some of their treasures for this purpose. A great deal of antique silver plate has already been sold for this very reason, but permission to do so has to be obtained from a Consistory Court, and even when that has been granted there are still a great many people who think that such sale is both sacrilegious and a breach of trust with the donors. There is, of course, a difference between selling silver vessels used for sacramental purposes and pieces of furniture used in the church for ordinary purposes. But where does one draw the line? If antique tables, chairs and stools are removed from the chancel, it will not be long before the Jacobean altar rails and the fourteenth-century carved pew-ends go as well, thus stripping the church of much historical interest. Most of these things have been given or left to the church through the ages, for a specific use. They were made by devoted craftsmen, not merely for gain, but because they loved their work and infused something of themselves into it. These things are part of the heritage of the place, and should remain there for the encouragement of generations of future craftsmen who might chance to see them. D. H. Lawrence expressed this feeling very well when he wrote:

Things men have made with wakened hands, and put soft life into, are awake through years with transferred touch, and go on glowing for long years. And for this reason some things are still lovely, warm still with the life of forgotten men who made them.

10 Old Recipes for Cleaning Antiques

Furniture Cleaner

Add 3 tablespoonsful of raw or boiled linseed oil, and 2 tablespoonsful of turpentine to 1 quart of water. Apply with a soft cloth to a small bit at a time, and then dry with a second cloth.

Furniture Polish and Cleaner

Fill a small bottle with equal parts of linseed oil, turpentine and vinegar and a small quantity of methylated spirits. Shake these until thoroughly mixed, and shake well before using. Rub in thoroughly with a piece of soft cloth, and polish well with a clean duster.

Furniture Polish

Put into a pan 2oz of yellow bees-wax and ½ pint of boiled linseed oil. Stand this in another pan full of boiling water till the wax is all melted, strain it, and when cool add 1 gill each of spirits of turpentine and vinegar, mix well together. Apply very thinly with a piece of flannel, rub again with another clean flannel, and finish with an old silk handkerchief.

An ideal duster is made of a soft chamois leather wetted and wrung dry. It can be used on the finest furniture, and gives a clean, bright surface. It completely removes finger marks. When the leather is wrung completely dry it does not damp the furniture.

Somes Useful Hints

Gilt, Lacquer and Treen

To clean this, use a white vegetable wax. This cleans as well as polishes. Be very sparing with it, and apply with a very soft cotton rag, or cotton wool, polishing with soft cloths afterwards.

Wax Polished Furniture

To clean wax polished furniture, such as dining-table tops that need washing, first use a cloth dampened with a mixture of vinegar and water. Rub dry with clean warm cloths and apply polish when quite dry.

Bamboo Furniture

This should be cleaned and polished by being washed with a solution of warm water and salt. Rub very dry with soft cloths.

'Grained-oak' Furniture or Panelling

Soak a piece of flannel with a little linseed oil, and rub the woodwork with it. Afterwards polish with soft cloths.

Glossary

Bazaar Small booths or stands in a hall, place of amusement or arcade in Regency London where fancy antiques of all kinds could be obtained. The Pantheon in Oxford St, London, was a notable example. The Edwardian 'penny bazaars' were a survival of this practice.

Brad Thin, flat, slightly-headed nail, used in shoemaking and picture framing.

Chamfer The bevel on the corner of a piece of furniture or on one side of a square leg.

Charger Large dish or plate of wood or metal for the serving of food.

Châtelaine A set of short chains attached to a medallion with a hook for clipping on to a woman's belt. Each chain carried a different useful object such as scissors, pencil, needlecase, note-pad, etc. Usually made of metal such as cut-steel or silver.

Chestnut-urns Two-handled urns in which hot chestnuts were kept. Usually made in pairs to stand on a sideboard, and manufactured chiefly of decorated lacquered tin at the factories at Pontypool and Usk in Wales.

Chip-carving Simple ornamental carving made with a chisel or gouge.

Escutcheon The name given to the metal or ivory plate surrounding a key-hole.

Etui A very small decorative case of metal, tortoiseshell or shagreen in which an amazing number of small implements for toilette or embroidery were kept such as folding-scissors, needle-case, scent-bottle, stiletto and ear-spoon. The inside of the lid was often fitted with mirror glass. The whole being no more than 1in × 2in.

Feather-banding A banding used as decoration for a piece of furniture, in which two pieces of inlay with the grain cut on the slant were placed side by side with the grain going in opposite directions, so that a 'feather' or 'herring-bone' effect was produced.

Feet (1) Bracket. This type of foot for furniture, small boxes, etc, was introduced in the eighteenth century and was formed by two bracket-shaped pieces of wood being joined (at the straight side) to form a corner foot.

(2) Bun, onion, pad and club feet are all shaped as their name implies.

Legs Cabriole. This type of leg swells out immediately below the piece into which it is fitted, and curves in again towards the foot.

Misericords Folding seats used in choir stalls, which when turned back disclose a ledge underneath supported by carvings. This ledge is wide enough for the singer to perch on when elderly or infirm.

Skillet   A long-handled pan of bronze or bell-metal on three legs, made for standing in the embers of an open hearth in order to heat milk, etc. The name of the maker, or a text, is often cut along the length of the handle.

Spindle   A thinly turned rod often tapered, used in the backs of chairs.

Stay-busks   These were made, chiefly in the eighteenth century, of wood, horn, bone or whalebone. They were slipped into a special pocket in the front of the shift or chemise, to give a straight effect to the corsage. They went out of fashion when the skimpy high-waisted dresses of the early nineteenth century came into fashion.

Stretchers   The pieces or rungs which connect the legs of chairs and tables.

Tambour-frame   An embroidery-frame originally formed by two long U-shaped pieces set across each other, which held the ring at the top on which the canvas was stretched. It was held on the knee, and thus allowed the use of both hands in making the tambour-stitch.

Templet   A cut-out pattern showing the outline from which the workman has to execute his work.

Treen = of trees   The name given collectively to small articles made of wood, either carved or turned.

Tun dish   A funnel, originally of wood, but can also be made of copper or brass.

Wheel-back   The name given to the type of Windsor chair which has a wheel carved out in the middle of the central splat.